TAKE JOY!

The Saga of Seagull Island

by

The Rev. Shuma Chakravarty

written in the voice of CRISPIN QUILPEN

"I believe that a simple and unassuming life is best for everyone, best both for the body and the mind."
Albert Einstein.

"Shuma you were always a poet. This book is a heartfelt and lovingly composed collection of tales which remind us to cherish our Mother Earth and Her many citizens."
Prentiss H. Knowlton.

ISBN: 978-0-9858282-9-5
Copyright © Shuma Chakravarty 2013

Published by:
CONVERPAGE
23 Acorn Street
Scituate, MA 02066
www.converpage.com

Acknowledgements

I wish to thank my publisher Pamela McCallum. I wish to thank Craig Smith for his editorial expertise and his technical assistance. I wish to thank Dr. Janice Marie Johnson for writing the preface of this book. I wish to thank Jill Christensen of MT for her moral support and generous friendship over the years. I wish to thank the Rev Elizabeth Wheatley Dyson for her moral support and generous friendship. The descriptions of this book by several scholars were written in May, 2013.

I wish to thank Dr. Margaret Studier, Managing Editor of *The Harvard Theological Review,* for her moral support and generous friendship over the years. I wish to thank Laura Whitney, Librarian of *Harvard Divinity School Library* for her moral support of my altruism and her gracious interest in my scholarly work.
I wish to thank the *Schlesinger Library of the Radcliffe Institute for Advanced Study,* Harvard University for its gracious interest in my scholarly work. I have happy memories of this library when I was a work-study student there in the late 1980's when I was a graduate student at Harvard Divinity School.

I wish to thank computer scientist Dr. Prentiss H. Knowlton of CA for his appreciation of my books and essays and for his description of this book. Finally, I wish to thank Thomas P. Marsan for his generous hospitality and his intuitive understanding of me as a mystic, pilgrim and poet.

"Now you belong to Heaven and the stars spell out your name" is from "Candle in the Wind" sung by Elton John at Princess Diana's funeral in 1997. The words are by Bernie Taupin. Princess Diana knew and revered Mother Teresa and died a few weeks before Mother Teresa's demise.

Reflections

"But do you really mean, sir," said Peter," that there could be other worlds
-- all over the place, just round the corner--like that ?"
" Nothing is more probable," said the Professor.
C.S. Lewis, *The Lion, the Witch and the Wardrobe.*

" It takes one a long time to become young."
Pablo Picasso.

"... we have...
Only begun to envision how it
might be live as siblings with
beast and flower ..."
Denise Levertov, "Beginners."

I recommend this book to all denizens of Tolkein's Shire, C.S. Lewis's Narnia and Melisande's marvellous worlds (of which the newest resident is Reepicheep's cousin, Mr.Marmaduke Montgomery Milkins).

Melisande's Chronicler,
Crispin Quilpen

"In the midst of winter, I finally learned that there was in me an invincible summer."

Albert Camus

" A book should serve as an axe for the frozen sea within us."

Franz Kafka

Author's Notes

Shuma Chakravarty is a minister, scholar and a published author of four books. Her poetry and prose have been included in several anthologies. She has graduate degrees in English Literature (from Simmons College) and Theology from Boston University and Harvard University. She is grateful for Nobel laureate, Professor Elie Wiesel's generous appreciation of her life and work ever since she became one of his students in 1978.
She was fortunate to have known Mother Teresa for many years and to have been greatly loved by her.

Foreword to *Take Joy!*

Each generation needs its oasis of peace, a place where one can only imagine a hope filled future even amidst the conflicts and dangers of the current culture. *Take Joy* is that spiritual oasis, where the reader can find peace, comfort and guidance to help live a different way, that this present world might become more like Seagull Island.

The Rev. Elizabeth Wheatley Dyson
Rector of St. Andrew's Episcopal Church
17 Church St.
Hanover, MA 02339

Preface to *Take Joy!*

by Dr. Janice Marie Johnson
Director of Multicultural Ministries and Leadership
Multicultural Growth and Witness of the
Unitarian Universalist Association.

When a calm, loving voice is needed to make sense of our ever so fragile world, the Rev. Shuma Chakravarty brings that voice, enveloping us in tenderness. In this precious volume, we are reminded of the universal power of ministry in its many disguises.

We are blessed to have the depth and breadth of wisdom that Rev. Shuma offers from the rich, lived-experience: the written word, the poetic word, and the compassionate word.

No matter how dangerous the night, this volume assure us of the coming of a grace-filled dawn.

Dawn
by Shuma Chakravarty

Sometimes the epiphany of pain
Announces the advent of Your presence,
Slicing my heart
With its tumultuous surge!

But my mourning turns into morning
When the sea-swell subsides,
Leaving only the
Opalescence of Dawn!

I wish to dedicate this book to my very generous and hospitable parents Uma Devi and Judhajit Kumar Chakravarty

And to the Multicultural Ministries and Leadership Department, Multicultural Growth and Witness of the Unitarian Universalist Association

and to
Mother Teresa (1910 -1997)
who often asked me " to do small things
with great love " and to do
"something beautiful for God."

"Now you belong to Heaven
And the stars spell out your name."

In 1975, then Prime Minister of India, Indira Gandhi wrote an insightful description of Mother Teresa.

The following is an excerpt from that article by Indira Gandhi about Mother Teresa:

"Who else in this wide world reaches out to the friendless and the needy so naturally, so simply, so effectively?
Tagore wrote ' there rest Thy feet where live the poorest, the lowliest, and lost.' That is where Mother Teresa is to be found--with no thought of, or slightest discrimination between colour or creed, language or country.
She lives the truth that prayer is devotion, prayer is service. Service is her concern, her religion, her redemption.
To meet her is to feel utterly humble, to sense the power of tenderness, the strength of love."

Dear Shuma

The fruit of SILENCE is Prayer
The fruit of PRAYER is Faith
The fruit of FAITH is Love
The fruit of LOVE is Service
The Fruit of SERVICE is Peace

Mother Teresa

God bless you
lee Teresa m c

Author's Foreword

This book is meant to be a Story for All Ages. I have invented parables, allegory, myth, fiction, included a few actual facts (about the plight of the environment of this planet) but used mainly the power of my imagination to create the luminous, peaceful realm of Seagull Island, where Wisdom guides all beings through Her mercy, melody and mirth. Seagull Island, ringed by the Singing Sea, as well as the Forest of Mirth, are imaginary oases under the loving, creative direction of Melisande, who in this book is none other than the divine essence of Wisdom. I chose the name Melisande only for its melodic quality. However, this character in my book has no connection with the medieval queen or with Debussy's operatic creation or with modern, fictional depictions of witches or heroines called Melisande.

Any resemblance to any being, factual or fictional, past or present, in this book, is purely coincidental and unintended. This book is a creation of the author's imagination. I will not lessen the reader's pleasure by disclosing in this preface details about Crispin Quilpen, the main narrator of this saga. ("Crispin's Tale" is at the end of this book). Suffice it to say that I created this benign being who lives in Wisdom's sanctuaries, imagined in this book. I hope that Crispin's voice will have the freshness of a spring morning as well as the ageless, perennial beauty of the vernal season of seeming rebirth, growth and gladness.

I dedicate this book to my mother, Uma Devi Chakravarty whose unconditional love continues to be the guiding light of my life.

I thank Craig Smith for his excellent technical assistance.

I regard the letter by Fra Giovanni, written in 1513, to be the prelude to this book. I hope that Fra Giovanni's radiant words may bring inspiration to all the readers of *Take Joy: The Saga of Seagull Island*.

Shuma Chakravarty,
Spring 2013.

Author's Notes

The Rev. Shuma Chakravarty has been the minister of several Unitarian Universalist churches in MA, and some United Church of Christ churches in MT and CA. She is currently the Director of The Resource Center for Ecology, Compassion, and Culture.

Author's Preface.

This book began ten years ago. I wrote it in the middle of a severe winter. The combat in Iraq had just begun and I was physically unwell due to a back injury. To escape the pain, both physical and emotional, instead of taking tablets, I relied on inspiration. When I felt inspired after prayers and meditations, I would write this book.
When the inspiration faded, I would not write until it returned. Therefore, these pages were only written when I was deeply filled with the awareness of God's grace. This book was in a manuscript edition but now it is finally published.

The global environmental situation is much worse now than it was a decade ago. Many more species have become extinct and the endangered list is much longer now. The global population today is more than seven billion people and climate change is a frightening fact. Wars are still raging in many places on this small planet. The chasm between people of wealth and financially poor people has increased significantly in this difficult decade.

Why, then, am I publishing this book now? I have finally found a suitable publisher. Also, the message of caring and sharing and living in harmony with humans and with other species on this planet is now no longer a choice but a *necessity for human survival, both collectively and individually.* As Denise Levertov wrote in her poem called *Beginners,* over thirty years ago:

> " ... *we have only begun ...*
> *to envision what it might be*
> *to live as siblings with beast and flower,*
> *not as oppressors.*"

I hope this book and its message of finding joy through genuine caring and sharing of our resources with all creatures on this small, blue planet will find some receptive readers.

Take Joy!

Shuma Chakravarty
Spring, 2013.

Take Joy!
Letter from Fra. Giovanni, 1513

*I am your friend
and my love for you goes deep.
there is nothing I can give you
which you have not got,
but there is much, very much
that while I cannot give it,
you can take it.*

*No heaven can come between us
unless our hearts find rest in today.
Take heaven!
No peace lies in the future
which is not hidden
in this present little instant.
Take Peace!
The gloom of the world is but a shadow.
Behind it,
yet within our reach
is joy.
Take Joy!*

*There is radiance and glory
in the darkness
could we but see –
and to see we have only to look.
I beseech you to look!*

*Life is so generous a giver,
but we, judging its gifts
by the covering,
cast them away as ugly,
or heavy or hard.
Remove the covering
and you will find beneath it
a living splendor,
woven of love,
by wisdom with power.*

*Welcome it, grasp it,
touch the angel's hand
that brings it to you.
everything we call a trial,
a sorrow, or a duty, believe me,
that angel's hand
is there,
the gift is there, and the wonder
of an overshadowing presence.
Our joys, too, be not
content with them as joys.
they, too, conceal diviner gifts.*

*Life is so full
of meaning and purpose,
so full of beauty
- beneath its covering-
that you will find earth
but cloaks your heaven.*

*Courage, then, to claim it,
that all is all.
But courage you have,
and the knowledge that
we are all pilgrims together,
wending through*

*unknown country, home.
And so, at this time,
I greet you.
Not quite as the world
sends greetings,
but with profound esteem
and with the prayer
that for you
now and forever,
the day breaks
and the shadows flee away.*

Foreword to the pictorial section of *Take Joy:*
The Saga of Seagull Island.

I am pleased to offer you this pictorial journey which will give you an idea of the beauty of Seagull Island, the Singing Sea and the Forest of Mirth, all of which were created by Melisande's joy and are sustained by Her music of mercy, melody and mirth.

I have only chosen pictures of Nature that can be found on Planet Earth.

Depictions of Melisande, Her children, the Shape-Shifters, the Mer and Fairy Folk are best left to the power of the imagination. I wish to thank Lise Beane for designing in 2003, the cover of this segment of *Take Joy: the Saga of Seagull Island.* I wish to thank the many photographers (who want to remain anonymous) for donating photographs taken between ten to thirty years ago. I thank them for their moral support of my altruism and for sharing their gifts of photography. My grateful thanks to everyone whose encouragement and enthusiasm brought this book to fruition in the Season of Splendor of Seagull Island, Spring 2013 on Planet Earth.

Wishing all beings Peace, Joy and Love,
Amen.

Crispin Quilpen,
Spring, 2013.

Crispin's Comments:

The last three pictures in the pictorial section will give you glimpses of the cuisine of Seagull Island. The colorful stew consists of a medley of garden vegetables. The fruit squares are topped with cream and fresh berries. The round, carrot cake is covered with cream and decorated with orange slices and walnuts in the shape of butterflies. All these dishes are very popular in Melisande's realms. Healthy and delicious meals are happily prepared and cheerfully served in Seagull Island for the enjoyment of all.

TAKE JOY

The Saga of Seagull Island

By Rev. Shuma Chakravarty

Glimpses of the Singing Sea

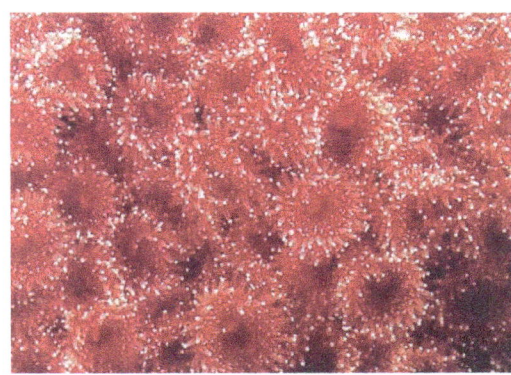

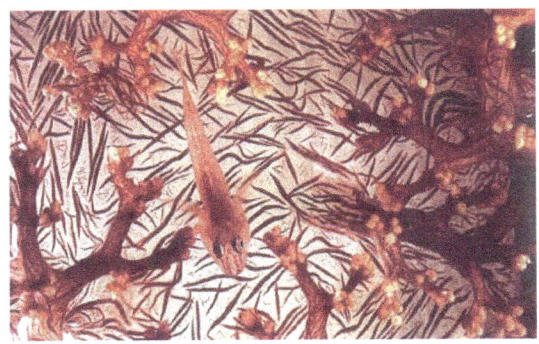

Savory Baked Vegetable Stew

The Saga of Seagull Island

Long ago, there was an island covered with sunflowers, edged with seashells of every stripe and surrounded by singing birds. Sailors called it "Seagull Island" for only seagulls had ever been seen to land or leave that island. Usually, a silvery sea mist shielded that isle from human view. But the island itself was a haze of green–gold to those who lived there. Golden corn and grain covered its fields and its forests were always green of many hues. Trees and shrubs, rivers and streams, fish and fowl, deer and pelicans lived as neighbors there without preying on each other, knowing there was an abundance for all. Seagulls, such shrill scavengers today, were makers of melody in those days, as they gracefully ringed that island, long ago. There were a few humans who also lived on that isle. They lived in little wattle-huts near the Singing Sea and learned early in their lives how to speak to the other inhabitants of that island. The sea, the flora and fauna and specially the seagulls and sunflowers each had their own song and humans alone on that island often spoke but seldom sang. But the human islanders knew that the other species there would only communicate with them and with each other through music. Any disharmony among humans there brought instant displeasure from the Singing Sea. As soon as it heard bickering, the Sea would send tumultuous waves surging around the shore and the Seagull Sentries would begin a symphony which would enrapture every hearer, whether bird or human, forest or flower.

You may well wonder how humans got there. The Seagull Sentries knew magic and when they saw a shipwreck, they became huge but invisible birds who carried humans to safety who would otherwise have drowned. Shipwrecks were rare in the Singing Sea and fortunately for all, there has not been a shipwreck off "Seagull Island" since the sixteenth century. Once the humans did arrive there they were first cared for by the fairy folk who filled the forests and streams of that island. The humans were taught to forget and forgive, to live and thrive and above all to be merry and kind. Sometimes it took years before they unlearned the lessons of the mainland. But until they could be truly kind, peaceful and helpful to all, they had to stay in training with the Fairy Folk in the depths of the forest. The name of that marvelous forest was Melisande but most beings on that island called it Berry Garden. Berries of every kind grew in succulent splendor in that forest. Strawberries, blackberries, gooseberries, blueberries and raspberries, currants of every hue and other edible berries unknown on the mainland, grew plentifully in the forest of Melisande. You may well ask who was Melisande? She was/is the essence of Wisdom whom the ancients Celts knew and loved. She had a singing laugh which had brought the beauty of all living beings in that forest to life, long ago. Even the moss and lichens, the stones and snails of that forest were very lovely, having been created by Melisande's laughter. She was only visible to those who truly loved Her. To all others She was warmth and wind, joy and water without which nothing can be truly alive. Melisande's garments were always green but usually covered with an abundance of blossoms of every season and every hue. She loved to dance and her slightest smile or movement was felt in the pulse of everything and everyone on that island as growth and goodness or simply the joy of life when it is full and fresh like a sunny, summer morning or a colorful day in autumn, full of fruit and flower!

Let me now tell you about a little boy named Jon Bray who lived on Seagull Island. His ancestors had come from two fascinating lands—ancient Ireland and medieval France. From Ireland he had inherited a ready wit and from France, his finesse. He was courteous to all with a hospitality that was always wholesome and warm. He gathered herbs, grains and vegetables; seeds, fruits and nuts from all over the island. Humans, birds and beasts alike enjoyed his soups and stews, cakes and ale. No one who came to his parents' door ever went away hungry. All were invited to sit and sup by sunlight, candlelight or firelight, whatever was seemly for the season or for the time of day. While his friends ate, Jon would regale them with jokes and stories that he had seen or heard or simply invented to brighten the moment with his *joie de vivre!* Jon loved to share a story about medieval France which I think you will really enjoy!

"Once upon a time during the reign of one of the King Louis (I forget the number) there lived in the village of Bray a family of farmers. In those days no one had a last name. People called each other only by their first names and sometimes they added the name of a place to show where they lived. This family was called de Bray which means of Bray or from Bray. Place names were particularly interesting in those days, for all names whether of a person, place or plant had a meaning. There was a man in Bray who owned a donkey who did all his errands. And it was the loud braying noise of the donkey which awoke the villagers every morning that gave the place its name. There was a forest near Bray which was almost as wonderful as our forest of Melisande. In that forest the animals were also fearless and led peaceful lives because they were guarded by a family of magical boars who were called Shape-Shifters because they could change their shape (or even vanish) at will. Boars had always lived in that forest ever since it came into being aeons ago, born of Melisande's smile. The forest here on Seagull Island is richer, fuller and even more wondrous because it came into being through Melisande's laughter.

The names of the farming couple were Claude and Marie of the village of Bray and they are my ancestors from medieval France. Very early one morning, before the donkey had brayed, farmer Claude was jolted awake by the hunting horns of the King's courtiers. Quickly pulling on an old coat and hat, Claude ran towards the sound. He arrived just in time to stop them from entering Melisande's forest with their bows and arrows. Kneeling on the ground, he told the king that this was not an ordinary forest but a magical sanctuary where birds and beasts spoke and thought, danced and sang, protected by the Shape-Shifters who were ageless guardians of the Forest; appointed by Melisande Herself.

"What would happen if we went hunting here? Do magic and miracles still occur here in our realm of France?" asked King Louis of farmer Claude. "You would be stitched in Time, Sire," answered the farmer. "Other days and years would come and go but you would always be stitched into this very moment of Time, thinking and speaking as if you were always here on the edge of this green wonderland. If any harm befell you, your Queen's river of tears would wash her golden tresses to gray before this sun sets today. But you, Sire, would not notice or care, always thinking you were here and she, far away, in her bower. The magical Boars cannot be killed, my lord, for they are Melisande's messengers. If you want fresh pork you can buy it cheaply from the village of Bray rather than enter this sanctuary with weapons."

The Saga of Seagull Island

The King looked pale on hearing this report. "Can any mortal enter this place?" he asked Claude. The farmer answered: "Yes, Sire but they must be free of any wish for violent sport and mortals can only come here if they really desire to live in harmony with Melisande's music. This melody cannot be just heard or taught but only lived. Only those who can live in harmony with birds, beasts and bees, leaf and flower, seasons and solitude, bounty and want, mercy and merry-making, truly at peace with flora and fauna, can come here . We mortals, Melisande says, are a motley mixture of earth and water, animal and angel, dung and divinity, chaos and star dust. She said that we are the youngest and least wise of Her own creation. Sometimes we have saddened Her and She has often wondered why in a moment of summer mirth She created so motley a mixture as mere mortals? There are no kings and courtiers in this forest only music and mirth, caring and sharing, working in unison with the many creatures born of Melisande's mirth."

The king looked at the farmer with surprised respect. He said: "You astonish me by your wisdom, living as I do surrounded by fops and fools. Tell me, whether this forest will offer me any food or drink this morning? These courtiers of mine are well wined and dined, even at this early hour. But I, their king, have been up since dawn, first reading, then signing, papers of state; then meeting with my ministers, then seeing an endless line of ambassadors from hither and yon. After that, I met with the Queen and sought her good counsel, for she is wise and unafraid to speak her mind to me. And then, I walked the royal poodles of France. Finally, I was fitted into these kingly garments. So you see, my man, I have not even eaten a croissant this morning while all these idle cads have been gorging and guzzling at my expense since dawn." The farmer replied: "I shall bring you a bountiful breakfast of fresh berries of every kind and spring water from this forest where I am always welcomed by Melisande's boars." Very soon the man returned with the berries and water, as he had promised. The king enjoyed his unusual breakfast very much and decided to create a duke out of the farmer. But Claude was concerned that this new honor would be a burden to him, not a blessing. He told the king that he was a man of few words and only spoke when there was a real reason to do so. The idle chatter of courtiers was not anything he knew or even wished to learn. The king then gave this farmer very special privileges.

Henceforth, Claude would be known as the Duke of Berry (not of Bray) and could sit in the royal presence wearing his smock and hat. If anyone greeted the new

Duke with a speech or expected him to do so, Claude could respond briefly, in his usual kindly way, using the word "Berry" in any sense he wished. For example Claude could say "Berry good" to most speeches and greetings or occasionally show disagreement by simply shaking his head and saying "Not berry." At Christmas time when there are greetings galore from every quarter, the new duke could only say "A very merry Berry" either by word or in writing. If he attended a wedding or christening all he had to say on leaving was "very Berry" i.e. "very good" (the capital B would be vocally expressed by a slight emphasis) and at funerals, the duke could express his sorrow by saying "VERY berry" (again the emphasis would be expressed by his verbal inflexion or nuance as the French so aptly say) i.e. "very sorry." If he wished to stop anyone he could stretch out his arm and say: "Berry" in a firm and commanding tone. If he wished to summon anyone, he could beckon to them and simply say: "Berry here," i.e. comes here. On meeting children or the aged, all the duke need say either at meeting or parting was "Berry" in a kindly tone, thus showing his approval, affection or even esteem. If a friend or colleague either from Bray or his new residence in Paris asked him how he was or his opinion of something, then the new duke with either a smile or a frown could simply say "Berry" with a Gallic gesture, thus indicating his joy or displeasure with the single, inflected word "Berry" and an expression which spoke volumes. If you think that Humpty Dumpty in Lewis Carroll's *Alice Through The Looking Glass* was the first to allow any word to mean anything he wanted, you are mistaken. That privilege was first given to my ancestor, Claude, the Duke of Berry, by King Louis of France.

When Claude ran home and told his wife Marie all about the adventures of that memorable morning, they decided **not** to forgo the solid security and known joy of their life as farmers of Bray for the vagaries and uncertainties of court life in the city. But they decided that every year they would spend the merry month of May on vacation from Bray at the King's court, as the Duke and Duchess of Berry. In their absence, the farm would be well taken care of by their nephew Jacques who was a sturdy lad and already in training as the farmer's heir. As a child he had been known as bonny Jon and now everyone called him honest Jack. Claude and Marie had a daughter whom they called Simone.

Let me tell you now about their farm in Bray. It was a delightful place where they had a variety of gardens. There was a walled herb garden filled with medicinal and flavorful herbs of many kinds. Their beautiful flower gardens were skillfully designed and tended. There were also large vegetable gardens and fruit orchards, a duck pond and a wonderful little hen house where the hens, roosters and their chicks lived. There were always fresh duck's and hen's eggs at their breakfast table and plenty of vegetables and fruits, both fresh and preserved, throughout the year. They bought milk from a dairy down the street and grains from their own farm were ground to make bread in their oven. Marie and Claude both liked to cook, so there was always plenty of butter and cheese, breads, cakes and pies, jams and jellies, fruit and vegetable preserves in their kitchen. Some of these were sold but they always left enough for their family, friends, neighbors and even passing strangers, all of whom they liked to feed. Their poultry were never killed or sold but kept in their family units. The mother ducks and hens always had plenty of their own eggs to hatch and were glad to give the farm family whatever eggs they needed to eat or to sell. The dairy farmers down the street also treated their cows, bulls and calves with kindness. The bulls helped the farmer with his ploughing, the calves played with the farmer's children and the contented cows gave enough milk to feed every calf and human in sight. So there was no shortage of cheese or butter or cream in the village of Bray. (I would not be surprised if the famous French "Brie cheese" originated in the village of Bray). Berries, however, were not grown in that village for they could be picked abundantly from the forest of Melisande who alone had the secret of berry-growing in France, at that time. Quite often the villagers of Bray would put a dollop of fresh cream over the berries as a special summer treat. Sugar was expensive in those days and tea and coffee were unknown but the fruits and berries were naturally, deliciously sweet, as were the fresh butter and cream which came from the milk of contented cows.

No fish, bird or animal was ever killed in Bray; no beast was maimed or mangled to suit human greed. No creature -- bird, beast or baby was turned into a plaything for anyone. That is why the people of Bray were such favorites of Melisande. Kings and presidents come and go, empires rise and fall but Nature prevails. The villagers of Bray were thought to be ignorant country bumpkins by the king's courtiers (and you know that they, in turn, were called fops and fools by their king) but the villagers were truly wise in knowing and loving what really matters even now (perhaps I should say, **specially now). The villagers of Bray knew that to be truly happy they must be in daily harmony with all that lives.** That was the simple secret of their wholesome joy and Melisande saw to it that the bounty of nature would nurture them and She protected them from nature's darkness. No floods, droughts, air or water borne disease ever harmed the villagers of Bray and they in turn never strained or severed their duty to be the peacekeepers of Melisande's multiple, motley, medley of Creation with its dominant music of mercy and mirth.

Melisande's messengers, the magic Shape-Shifters who guarded her French forest, sometimes took the guise of boars. Sometimes these spirits shook off that shape which then became a lifeless cloak (or should I say boar carcass?) and left it at night in the village green for the villagers to find and cook in the morning. Both the people of Bray and Melisande (whose mirth has brought everything into being whether we know it or not) knew that no living boar or pig had been killed for their fun and feasting. However, this magic meat was more delicious than anything from a hunt or a butcher's shop and thus Bray became famous and envied in all of France for its succulent pork! That is why, farmer Claude mentioned this village specialty to King Louis who had mistakenly imagined he could find this pork by hunting boars in Melisande's sanctuary, the Forest of Mirth."

Suddenly Jon Bray stopped his story. He said: "Why it is almost twilight! How I have rambled on about the past! Let's go at once to the beach here on Seagull Island."

There were no boats on Seagull Island. This surprising lack was due to the fact that stories of shipwrecks of distant days which were told and re-told to succeeding generations had left their mark. Secondly, no one wanted to leave Seagull Island and lastly, no islander ever fished, for *the Singing Sea was also one of Melisande's creations and therefore a sanctuary*. There were plenty of fish of many colors and designs, mer folk and dolphins who lived in the Singing Sea. If any child or farm duckling wanted a ride on the sea they could always call on their dolphin friends for assistance. Sitting on the smooth backs of the dolphins they would skim over the waves of the Singing Sea, softly murmuring its own music as they sailed. Adult humans here were good swimmers and often at twilight would dive into the Singing Sea to visit the mer folk who floated up at sunset to see the gold-pink sky. The Singing Sea itself was like a dazzling opal at the sunset hour. Tinged with vermilion and green, sapphire blue and scarlet by the rays of the setting sun, Melisande's Singing Sea at twilight, was truly a wonder to behold!

It is safe to say that mer folk, specially mermaids, have been mistakenly misrepresented in the myths of the mainland. Mermaids are usually depicted in such stories as brazen hussies whose siren songs lure innocent mariners in sailing ships to their doom. These stories also incorrectly portray mermaids as half human and half fish (from the waist down). While mermen in such stories are seen as sinister and cruel towards humans and quarrelsome to each other, **the truth is that mer folk are benign Shape-Shifters who are Melisande's artists of the deep.**

Have you noticed the exquisite fishes that are sometimes glimpsed in the Singing Sea? I have heard from the seagulls that even humans from the mainland never eat such fish, if they catch them in their nets but keep them in large, well lighted aquariums, tending and feeding them fresh fish food, so that the beauty of those exquisite fish can be seen and admired by many! It is the mer folk who design and paint such fish with orange and silver, yellow and blue colors, sometimes placing feathery fins on them and sometimes adding a single, round, black dot to decorate these fish with a touch of "whimsy." Once the mer folk have finished designing and painting the miniature fishes, they call Melisande, for only Her mirth can breathe life into them.

You may well ask, what are mer folk really like? Like all of Melisande's creations they are merciful and merry, beautiful and blithe. When they are under water, they simply look like large fish. When they float upwards they assume human forms. But real humans and other creatures on Seagull Island know they are mer folk because their beautiful eyes look like opals, ever incandescent. Indeed all Shape-Shifters have opal-like eyes. But neither the mer folk nor the magical boars of that French forest ever seek to puzzle or delude any of Melisande's creatures with their Shape Shifting. They only change their shapes when it is necessary to do a special task for Melisande whether it be guarding a sanctuary or designing miniature fishes for Her joy.

Now let me tell you about another delightful child who lived on Seagull Island. His name was Pip Darcy and he was Fill Bray's best friend. His real name was Philippe d'Arc and his ancestors had also come from medieval France, actually from the same village of Arc (in French, d'Arc) as the famous warrior martyr St. Joan (in French St. Jeanne d'Arc). Philippe's mother Marie loved English literature. Consequently, her son's nick name became Pip Darcy. Pip from Dickens' novel *Great Expectations* and Darcy from Jane Austen's classic *Pride and Prejudice*.

Did you know that the residents of Seagull Island whether flora or fauna, fish or forest, humans or mer folk, all believe that the greatest word wizard in the English language, namely William Shakespeare (b. 1564-d.1616) was lent to England by his mother Melisande ? She knew that this excellent Shape-Shifter from Her forest sanctuary (and a lover of Her Singing Sea) would create poetry and plays that would be cherished by humanity for hundreds of years. After fifty two years in England, Shakespeare returned forever to Melisande's world and even now he can sometimes be seen at dawn or dusk, as a silvery sheen on the waves of the Singing Sea. (Now you know why some of the Seagull Islanders love English literature, since one of their own, namely, Shakespeare graced and gladdened the English language forever).

What did Pip look like you may well ask? Pip was a tow headed tyke with sparkling blue eyes, a round rosy face and cherry red lips, on which he usually wore a merry grin. When he was a baby, his mother Marie had washed his eyes with the sweet waters of the Singing Sea. Ever since then, there was sparkle in his eyes and a song or smile on his cherry mouth. His mother being French, sometimes called him *cheri* (dear). But most people, specially his pals, called the little boy either Pip or Cherry. We will simply refer to him as Pip in this story.

Pip's mother had left a basket of fresh peaches on Seashell Beach for the children to enjoy during the twilight hour when they came to watch the beauty of sunset in their Singing Sea. Suddenly, Pip asked Jon and all their friends to sit in a circle on the beach while he handed them the peaches and sang and danced for their delight.

Pip sang:

"I am a little, bouncy boy kin but many names have I!
I am too young for sherry, though my mother calls me cheri,
My pals call me Cherry and a Merry boy, Pip, Pip, Pippin am I."

Then he said: "Sometimes in my dreams I see the village of Arc in medieval France. I often imagine sweet Saint Jeanne tending her father's flock of sheep, singing or hearing angels in her visions and finally being burned by horrible fools but her spirit soared above the flames and became a white dove which lives in Heaven. Did you know that Saint Jeanne is beloved of Mother Marie and of course of Melisande? That is my story about medieval France. Now Jon must finish his story."

Jon continued: "April was the month for journeys to shrines in medieval Europe and also in England. You remember, I am sure, Chaucer's *Canterbury Tales*. But May, though dedicated to Mother Mary, was a merry month for mortals, filled with fun, frolic and feasting. It was in May that every village had a maypole in its green center and colored ribbons were tied to the top of the maypole and streamed down, so that every village lass and lad could dance around it, each holding a bright ribbon. It was in May that even the King and his court went on picnics to the countryside and the Queen was often given a crown of flowers when she went berry picking in the forest with her ladies. Wandering minstrels sang and played their lutes and mandolins to entertain courtiers and villagers alike. Pastry chefs made a fortune turning forest fruits into tortes and tarts for the king's and queen's repast and their courtiers' delicious delight! Very often church bells announced weddings, for many a lass and lad were married in the merry month of May. Everyone danced at weddings. Peasants danced on the village green and in the king's court dances called polkas and pavanes were particularly popular in the merry month of May. Weddings were always celebrated outdoors in May. As soon as the church service was over, the bride and groom and their families and guests were seated at splendid banquets that were held outdoors. Flowers and fruits were always plentiful, then and now, in the merry month of May. No wonder my ancestors, Claude and Marie of Bray chose the month of May to holiday in the king's court as the Duke and Duchess of Berry! Due to their influence and in their honor, forest berries became very popular at court and the king's cooks vied with each other to create many delicacies based on berries. A medley of berry jams and jellies, pies and preserves filled the royal pantry and wonderful dishes such as berry soufflés, berry fondues, berry tarts and berry tortes graced the king's feasts regularly in May. Even the Queen's May flower crown had berries placed in it to add to its beauty and fragrance! You can imagine that the farming couple, my ancestors Claude and Marie, now the new Duke and Duchess of Berry, thoroughly enjoyed every moment of the merry month of May at the royal court! But after a while, the jugglers and jesters, cooks and clowns no longer looked as entrancing as they did at the very beginning of their leisure time. Though still delighted with everyone and everything, Claude and Marie were actually glad to return to their farm in Bray on the very last day of the merry month of May. They maintained this pattern for many years i.e. farming in Bray for eleven months and vacationing at the royal court as a duke and duchess during the month of May. One day, when they were advanced in years, though still keen of mind and vigorous of body, they decided to retire, both from the farm (which would now be run by their nephew Jacques) and from the May court of King Louis as well.

Having faithfully loved and served Melisande for many years as Her stewards, Claude and Marie requested Her to send them (via magical means) to Seagull Island. Very few mainland mortals know of this island but Melisande had once mentioned this sanctuary, knowing that Claude and Marie would never violate Her trust or share this sacred secret with anyone else. Only their daughter Simone was allowed to accompany them to Seagull Island. Instead of undergoing the ordeal of a shipwreck, Melisande arranged for three of Her magical sentries to fly Claude, Marie and Simone on birds' beaks to Seagull Island. Now you know as much about this family as I do! Oh, need I add that they all lived happily ever after? My father did not want to be always linked to forest berries, ancestral or otherwise. He decided to reclaim the former name (or rather, the original place name of Bray), so my name is Jon Bray."

Everyone thanked Jon for finishing his story and as the sunset hour was ending, the children walked back to their respective homes (or should I say cosy wattle huts?) on Seagull Island's Seashell Beach.

Since we were all children once, I think it is safe to say that most people are interested in knowing something about children, specially those who live in unusual or exotic places such as Seagull Island.

The Saga of Seagull Island

As soon as a baby was born in Seagull Island, the father of the child or a grandparent waded into the sweet waters of the Singing Sea carrying aloft a colored, lighted candle. Then the following song would be sung or chanted:

"Mighty Mother Melisande,
Full of mirth and mercy,
On Your maiden reindeer, come,
Bringing bliss and benison!
Come and meet, greet and guide,
This our newest baby kin."

As soon as this was sung, Melisande magically arrived. Her garments were always green of many hues and often covered with the blossoms of the season. She had a reindeer and a fawn on either side and a snowy, baby seagull was perched on Her smooth, right shoulder. The little seagull carried a glowing yellow sunflower in its baby beak which Melisande always gave to the baby's mother as She blessed the babe. You will not be surprised to learn that Melisande was the godmother of all beings who were born on Seagull Island. Piglets and ducklings, fluffy yellow chicks, dappled fawns, baby birds, saplings, rosebuds, little dolphins and, of course, all human infants were Her own godchildren. Melisande, whose mirth has brought all creation to life, was a superb godmother to all growing beings and Her tender mercy filled them with vibrant joy and goodness, like rays of clear sunlight which have to be experienced rather than described.

I am sure that you will ask: "And then?" So let me share with you what I know about the nature and nurture of the children of Seagull Island or to put it primly, the upbringing and education of the young humans of that isle. But some essential details must come first. The babies of Seagull Island, all of whom lived in their parents' cosy wattle huts on Seashell Beach were first fed on their mothers' milk, then on the milk of contented cows and they also drank plenty of sweet water which their parents brought from the Singing Sea. After that, the children of this island shared their parents' diet of an abundance of fresh fruits and vegetables, eggs, milk, butter and cheese, breads of many kinds, nuts and grains, lentils, berries, cakes and corn. They also ate a variety of soups, salads and stews, pies and pastries and many other wholesome dishes whose names I have forgotten now. As you know, Melisande's marvelous Will (whom we know as Shakespeare) had been lent to the mainland for 52 years. When he returned, Will brought back (in his memory) a wide array of recipes from olde England which he introduced to the inhabitants of Seagull Island. Syllabubs and syrups, pasties and puddings, gooseberry fool (a dessert), spotted dick (another dessert),scones, custards, crumpets, cream puffs, strawberries and clotted cream, hot cross buns, sandwiches, trifles, turnovers, popovers, biscuits, hot buttered toast, Yorkshire pudding, Bubble and Squeak, Toad-in-the-hole, Shepherds' pies and Christmas puddings are only some of Will's many culinary imports ! You are probably wondering if the islanders' diet excluded fish, poultry and red meat. Although the sanctity of all forms of life was respected in Melisande's worlds, the Shape- Shifters (the best of whom was William Shakespeare himself) saw to it that no human being on Seagull Island lacked the taste of fish or meat, if they desired to eat that. Most islanders had long outgrown any longing for the slain flesh of fish, beast or of bird but the few in whom there was this residual wish could have an abundance of charmed food which the Shape - Shifters had created out of grains and nuts to magically taste like pork or venison, lobster or caviar or any dish of any other meat or fish anyone wanted to eat. When Dryden, (an English author), first read Chaucer's works he is believed to have said: "Here is God's plenty!" In the same vein, I can truthfully tell you that there was always an abundance of healthful, delicious food in Melisande's sanctuaries!

 Now the next inevitable question will be asked: "What did they drink?" This is easy to answer, I am glad to say. The soil of Melisande's magical Seagull Island welcomed any benign seed that was planted in it. Consequently, the islanders could drink a variety of fruit and vegetable juices as well as spring water from the streams and the sweet water of the Singing Sea. If this was not enough, a multitude of teas, coffees and cocoa grew on this isle as well as green coconuts which contain a delicious, clear water inside the hard shell of the tender, young coconuts. Some of the human islanders made cider as well as lemonade. And the Berry family had concocted a delicious drink made out of a variety of fresh, forest berries that they bottled and sold as "Very Merry Berry." So, you see, here again on Seagull Island, there was a delicious, healthful abundance of beverages for humans of all ages and tastes. Now we finally come the important issue of the "upbringing" of the island's children (or how they were raised). As you know by now, everyone on Seagull Island had to live in daily harmony with all that lives in

Melisande's sanctuaries. This is a lesson that most people on the mainland do not wish to learn. Here, on Seagull Island it had been very difficult for rescued mariners to unlearn the lessons of hatred but after many years in Melisande's forests, the patient fairy folk had finally taught these people how to care and share. As I have told you before, there has **not** been a shipwreck off Seagull Island since the sixteenth century. Therefore, the humans here have learned to live peacefully for centuries now and their children are naturally in tune with Melisande's music of mercy and mirth, living in harmony with all of Her motley, medley of marvelous Creation!

Have you wondered why the phrase "a school of fish" was coined? Surely a "shoal of fish" would be more accurate; just as "an exaltation of skylarks" needs no explanation. Well, this little mystery will soon be solved when I tell you that one of the school rooms of the children of Seagull Island was indeed under the Singing Sea. The children went there under the supervision of several Shape -Shifters who transformed them for an hour into exquisite, painted fishes. This was their "Nature study, under water class" and the benign Shape-Shifters, (the greatest of whom was Shakespeare himself), simply wanted the children to understand and experience at first hand the beauty of the sea and its exquisite life forms, one of which is its miniature "painted fish."

The children of this isle had plenty of time on land and they thoroughly enjoyed the wealth and wonder of Melisande's Seagull Island. They loved learning from their own parents how to read and write. They learned from the seagulls and the Singing Sea much about music. In the forest, the children found the fairy folk who taught them **the secrets of wholesome joy, i.e. how to live in daily harmony with bird and bee, flora and fauna, humans and mer folk, forest and field, sun and sky**. They learned to cook and bake, build and paint and a medley of many practical tasks from their parents and neighbors. Thus, at a fairly young age, the children and youth of Seagull Island were blest with many opportunities to blossom into kind, capable people with excellent skills and insights. There was no school graduation in this island, for as long as they lived, the beings there delighted in increasing their store of knowledge in order to help each other and thus add to Melisande's mirth.

On occasion, but not very often, there was an Honored Guest on Seagull Island. Let me tell you what I know about an Indian parrot of spring- leaf -green plumage, scarlet beak, bright black, beady eyes and a brilliant brain whose full name was Sri Sri

Prem Chand Mitra. This roughly translated is The Very Revered Love Moon Friend. This parrot, however, was rather shy about disclosing the meaning of his fulsome name and always told everyone he met: "You will only mispronounce my name. Just call me Mr. P. or P. for short." This parrot was by inclination and training a logician and a lawyer, specializing, of course, in **Non-human Species Protection Advocacy** which he had studied in depth and in detail in Delhi and Deradoon, Dresden and Dusseldorf, as well as in California, Florida, Bermuda, London and the Seychelle Islands. So you can see, at a glance, that Parrot P. had a resume that was really impressive and even excellent! There was nothing lyrical, mystical or even melodic in P.'s temperament. The swift clicking of an efficient typist best resembles this Parrot's punctual and precise mind. After graduating with highest honors from fifteen law schools in fifty countries (which provided specialized training in his field i.e. **Non-human Species Protection Advocacy**), this erudite Indian parrot decided to do further research in several places. His advanced studies took him first to Delhi, then to Dhaka, then to Durban, Derby, Dublin, Derry and Durham (both in the U.K. and in the U.S.A.) and finally to Denmark where he received the honor of being the first being (no pun or fun intended) to receive the Dahngold award which either equals or surpasses the Nobel prizes of Sweden and even the Nobel Peace Prize of Norway. The Dahngold is a medal given for **exemplary erudition**. And the Danes who love Nature, thought it only fitting that the very first holder of this title should be a non-human specialist in a particular form of **eco-jurisprudence**—a brilliant bird from the fading forests of India (a country renowned from ancient times for its wealth of spiritual wisdom).

As soon as the BBC and CNN included the above mentioned award in their breaking news, there was no rest or respite for Sri Sri Prem Chand Mitra who prefers to be called Mr. P., (short for Parrot). The "mainland", as Seagull Islanders calls our World, rushed to this parrot's perch, to coin a phrase. Sponsors of Female Human Beauty Contests emailed P. in India from California, asking him to pose on the shoulders of bikini clad, bathing belles for publicity photographs and even to be seen eating succulent strawberries from their hands, lips or even hips! P. was always offered enormous sums of money, including all travel expenses, nuts and fruits from certified health food stores and anti-kidnapping insurance as well. Bird sanctuary specialists promised to be this Parrot's hosts (and even hostages or human shields, in case of terrorist attacks by Bird Robbers for Billionaires, a newly formed, "foemented" and

*Sri Sri Prem Chand Mitra
Winner of The Dahngold Medal*

much feared group of shrewd gangsters, all of whom wanted to retire from crime at age thirty and start philanthropies and foundations instantly on retirement, in order to protect their ill-gotten wealth).

Some of the oldest, newest, largest and wealthiest universities in the U.K., U.S.A. and in the European Union offered Mr. P. professorships, fellowships, grants, tenure and sabbatical leave with pay, even before his actual arrival i.e. bribes and bonuses. These schools hoped and longed to become the first academic institution in the whole world to have ONE tenured, senior professor who was a non-human jurist in a special branch of **eco-jurisprudence** (which I have already described to you twice) AND the very first recipient of the Dahngold which was just created by Denmark to honor exemplary erudition, as you already know.

After all, the prestigious Nobel prize has been around, so to speak, for a long time; (at least a hundred years, I think). The Danes had watched for years these glittering, annual, Nobel ceremonies hosted by their neighbors in Sweden and in Norway, with seeming indifference. But suddenly, when the moment was finally ripe, when ecologists and environmentalists had reached global respectability and animal rights as well as human rights agendas (or only outlines of suggestions for humane actions) had been placed at last on the tables of presidents **and** their wealthy cronies by their own lobbyists, "spin doctors" and P.R. lawyers themselves, THEN, AND ONLY THEN, the Danes with exquisite timing (some say, timing as precise in planning, as their Viking raids of old) had invented the Dahngold medal of honor and bestowed it on a PARROT! Yes, a PARROT but a PARROT from INDIA who had demonstrated his **exemplary erudition**, to use the key phrase again from the Danish award, in every law school on planet Earth that had the sense and grant-getting savvy, to include a **Non-human Species Protection Advocacy Program** in its curriculum (or even to pay lip-service to this new field of **eco-jurisprudence** in its printed catalogues which are always carefully read by past, present and prospective donors).

What, you may well ask, were the responses of powerful and often erudite Swedes and Norwegians to the recent Danish medal of honor, the Dahngold? I am sorry to say that these neighbors of the Danes often called this medal that "darn gold" with bland faces until publicly, politely corrected by foreign journalists, visiting dignitaries or even diplomats. Then, these detractors of the Danes instantly said: "We mean the Dahngold medal, of course. You must not take umbrage at our innocent mispronunciation."

I did hear that in Cambridge, in the U.S.A. and in Cambridge in the U.K., where fairly large groups of Nobel laureates and their groupies can be found, a new group, (akin to **Save the Whales**) called **The Noble, Nobel and non-Nobel Prize Winners, Angry Anonymous Caucus Inc.** are already collecting signatures and donations to demonstrate world wide before Danish embassies (and even before all-American shops and stores where the U.S. breakfast fast food called Danish pastry is sold). Some members of this **Anglo-American Caucus**, who may even be Nobel laureates themselves, are already preparing lectures, papers, CDs, DVDs, films and monographs on "The Distinctions and Definitions of Denmark's Dahngold and its Global Significance." Several lecture topics, (which will soon be given at prominent universities in the U.K. and in the U.S.A. by Nobel laureates, hitherto disinterested in geography in general and Denmark in particular), have already been announced e.g. "What Denmark must mean to you, to me and to us for the safety of international erudition and the Anglo-American Alliance." "The Nobel or the Dahngold —both or either? Must a genius choose?" "Are the days of patrons over? Why and why not the Dahngold?" "I have a Nobel but must I stop there? I have not yet gone to Denmark for the Dahngold!" The four lengthy titles of these forthcoming lectures will give you an excellent idea of the mood of the **Caucus** which I have already described.

Not only academia but even the corporate world of **Businesses for Big Bucks** (often called the triple B), tried to buy Mr. P. and were not shy in their efforts to summon him. They thought he could be used to market many things AND to create further urges for consumption in gullible shoppers for items that they had hitherto neither wanted nor needed or even imagined! These items could be called, for example, **Parrot Pills for Mood Maintenance, for People of any gender, race, age or income; Parrot Beak-Red lipsticks for Pretty Pollys; Mr. P.'s Special Parrot After Shave Lotion for Fabulous Men; Parrot Prompt Ales for Sunny Seniors; Parrot Nut Snacks for Special Pets and Parrot Purees of Sweety Fruitys for Tiny Tots.** Food and beverage industry C.E.O.s had every intention of re-launching a whole line of their existing products under a new name and different packaging called **Parrot's Paragon Specials Supreme.** They, in turn, emailed Mr. P. with their offers, promising to make him the richest and best known, most photographed parrot in history, before the end of that very month! Fabulous sums of money and special perks were offered to Mr. P. by other equally enormous corporations who sought to outbid each other in their fierce attempts to purchase him.

Book publishers, best selling authors and even literary agents also offered Mr. P. huge advance payments of money just to be photographed for book covers with co-authors of forthcoming novels called: *The Parrot Speaks — who killed whom, where and when?* and *The loves and lives of sexy Parrots from Plato's Poly to Faulkner's Hoby.*

Movie industries also tried to capture Mr. P. For instance, Bollywood of India offered him indefinite, rent-free residence in a fake forest, movie set (made of green plastic) which was an imitation of his actual habitat in one of the fading forests of India. Bollywood reminded Mr. P. that their fake forest was in India, after all, and he could hear tapes of forest sounds when he started his residency in that movie set.

Hollywood, on hearing about this offer, was frankly alarmed! After a long meeting behind closed doors led by financiers, producers, directors, movie stars, members of their all -American movie crews' union etc.; a Hollywood spokesperson was finally chosen to convey a handsome counter-offer to Mr. P. Hollywood offered Mr. P. rent-free, life tenancy in a REAL forest of "just planted" trees which would resemble his original Indian habitat. This forest would cover one acre of a movie mogul's hundred acre California estate. This planted-to-order forest would be created by **Fresh, Fast, Forest Planters Inc.** of Southern California. This **F.F.F.P. Inc.** promised its clients "instant forests new or old." Its fliers stated that its "Forests can be quickly made to look antique by adding mud, mildew and live moths, for an additional fee. Custom designed fresh forests can also be planted for a small, flat fee of about $2 million per forest."

You may well ask how did countries in other climes and continents respond to Mr. P.'s success?

African countries asked Mr. P. to visit that continent at his own expense. However, on arrival, he would be introduced to shamans who would evaluate Mr. P.'s totemic potential. The Aborigines of Australia also invited Mr. P. to come Down Under on the same terms as the Africans but offered him the additional possibility of exploring Dream Time with them, as a special treat.

Suddenly, every group of indigenous people in Greenland, Iceland, Lapland, Newfoundland, every island off the coast of either side of the Americas; plus minority groups residing on the mainland of Canada, North, Central and South America as well as in Mexico and in Cuba, created quite legally (after consulting excellent lawyers from each country in these vast continents) The fully **United Nations of Ancient Peoples in the New Worlds.** They then sent songs and citations to Mr. P. in India. They also informed him that their soothsayers in olden days had prophesied the arrival and success of a Remarkable Bird (i.e. Parrot) from the East!

Alarmed by this sudden solidarity of many, marginal, minority groups; countries in Central and in South America created, again legally, **The New Solidarity of Iberians Here in this not so New World.** They used the word Iberian because Brazil, where Portuguese is spoken, might have felt excluded, if the words Hispanic or Spanish were exclusively used. Mexico and Cuba decided, on governmental levels, that this was the moment for all Iberians, of each and every ideology, in the not so New World, to make common cause against known or unknown foes. Suddenly, sombreros were worn by Iberian males of every age. And all female Iberians, again of every age, were always seen with lace mantillas on their heads. It was only during family or business visits to Spain and to Portugal that Iberians from the not so New World felt it was safe to wear unisex, U.S. jeans and tee shirts again and to speak English with American accents, while eating burgers and drinking coke. It was a matter of collective security, as well of Iberian honor, for every Iberian resident of the Americas to be as Latin as possible, in their speech, dress, eating and drinking habits, in short, in every aspect of their modus operandi while living in the not so New World !

You may be interested to know that a citation written in Spanish <u>and</u> in Portuguese was sent by email to Mr. P. in India from **The New Solidarity of Iberians Here in this not so New World.** An attachment was added to Mr. P's email from this group of Iberians which had a picture of a young, male guitarist serenading a young lady who was standing above him on a balcony with her grandmother as her duenna beside her. Both ladies were wearing lace mantillas, long dresses and carrying ornate fans in their gloved hands. A bright green parrot was sitting in a tree opposite the maiden's home observing everything. Such was the gracious tribute to Mr. P.'s sagacity and refinement, (as well as his erudition which was mentioned in the citation), by **The New Solidarity of Iberians Here in this not so new World!**

Since various sectors of the U.S.A. had already contacted Mr. P., the White House, as well as the Senate and Congress decided to send Mr. P. a collective email of brief but hearty salutations. The U.S. ambassador to India, they decided, needed to stay on in New Delhi in order to send frequent, soothing messages in person and by fax, phone, mail and email to government officials in India, Pakistan, U.S.A., Afghanistan, as well as to a variety of "war lords" whom many in India call "cross border terrorists."

Canada, Iceland, Lapland and Greenland sent official greetings to Mr. P. by email. It was made clear to Newfoundland authorities that a Canadian greeting included their interests and a similar note was sent to Quebec.

Chinese government officials thought Mr. P. should agree, without any fee, to be cloned. However, China would reserve all rights to sell his clones globally and to profit from that sale. A little bit of that clone-sale money, however, would be used for panda preservation, by conserving bamboo groves and even bamboo forests in mainland China!

The Millionaires' Club of Japanese Businessmen offered to pay all expenses for Mr. P.'s visit to Japan, as well as travel and food fees, if only Mr. P. agreed to live in a golden cage on the grounds of the Imperial Gardens in Tokyo during his Japanese visit and recite haikus (short poems) to the Imperial family. The Japanese government thought that the creation of a new award for Mr. P. would *not* befit their dignity, as representatives of an ancient civilization. However, they were willing to ask the Emperor's Chief Ornithologist (or human expert on birds) to award Mr. P. the **Golden Crane Medal for Honorable Scholarship**. Cranes, the Japanese officials argued, though not parrots, are birds, after all.

The Australian government, in close communication with all its major athletes, as well as members of its Sheeps' Fleece and Lamb Industry, decided to invite Mr. P. (all expenses paid, of course) to be a guest **Sport's Mascot**. Mr. P. would be asked to pose with major tennis and other sports' stars and those pictures would, in turn, be placed on tennis rackets and diverse sports' equipment, as well as on boxes of breakfast cereals. Mr. P. would be given a sporting fee or better still; a tax-deductible check could be given, on Mr. P.'s behalf, to the **International Association of Forest Protection Activists.** They are currently based in the Cayman Islands for tax shelter reasons or have they already moved to Monaco?

Prosperous Singapore sent Mr. P. a packet of bird seeds that their customs officials had recently confiscated from the luggage of a distinguished ornithologist from Eugene, Oregon, U.S.A. Her name is Ms. B. Grayson and she had come to Asia to attend birding walks, talks and a conference called **"Parrots—what do they mean to you and to me and to Global Ecology?"** I must tell you more later about Ms.

Grayson and her cousin, Dr. Duckworth. For now, all I need mention is her righteous wrath when her granola bars, trail mix and her last packet of bird seeds were suddenly seized by Singapore's custom officials who suspected that illegal drugs, disguised as health food, were in her backpack. She left Singapore, still clutching a bottle of spring water purchased in Vermont, U.S.A. Before she boarded her plane, a kind, young Singapuri customs officer brought her a double burger and fries. He had just purchased This food with his own money from the local Burger King. That for her was the final insult! Ms. Grayson momentarily lost her manners, then and there. She suddenly screamed: "You will hear from my cousin the surgeon, Dr. Duckworth of Florida, sir. I am a strict Vegan sir. Don't you dare insult me, sir?" When careful lab. tests disclosed that there were no narcotics, hidden or otherwise, in any of the confiscated items from Ms. Grayson's backpack, (including the sealed packet of bird seeds), the government officials of Singapore decided to repackage the bird seeds in a small, local, jute bag and send it to Mr. P. who was in India, at that time.

Myanmar (the country that used to be called Burma) sent Mr. P. an exquisite parrot's perch made of its famous teak wood. They also sent him a tiny Burmese, beak-red ruby on a gold chain which he could wear around his neck while (or should I say, if) visiting foreign or local heads of state, some of whom happen to be royalty.

Not to be outdone by its neighbor, Thailand sent Mr. P. a special medal, also shaped like a necklace. This award was called **The Celestial Elephant Prize** and a carved, jade pendant depicted the King of Thailand seated on an elephant who, in turn, was seated on a bank of clouds. The tiny, royal figure on this pendant was carrying an umbrella over his own as well as the elephant's head, presumably to protect both of them from rainfall (or was the open umbrella a sign of their joint sovereign importance in heaven and even on earth?). Mr. P. was informed that an ancient country like Thailand could **not** be expected to invent an honor, in order to compete with its western trade partners. They hoped that this award would further facilitate Indo-Thai economic and cultural partnerships in the present **and** in the future. **The Ornithology Association of Siam-Thailand** offered Mr. P. an honorary membership but waived the dues and stated that he would **not** be required to attend their monthly meetings (which involved visits to regional bird sanctuaries etc.).

Bhutan sent Mr. P. its prestigious **Royal Mountain Bird Award.** Nepal gave Mr. P. its **New Feathered Foreign Friend and Nice Near Neighbor Perpetual**

Pal Award. It also sent Mr. P. pictures of its past and present Nepalese royal families and a color photograph of Mt. Everest which included a group of young mountaineers sitting at its base, being blessed by Sir Edmund Hillary and by the descendants of the late Tenzing Norgay (i.e. the two original conquerors of Mt. Everest in 1953). Both these mountainous kingdoms to the north of India, Bhutan and Nepal, wanted Mr. P. to be their goodwill ambassador to India in particular and to the globe in general.

The kings, presidents and potentates of most Middle Eastern countries offered Mr. P. opportunities to come as their guest (all expenses paid, of course but under the human supervision of one of their own envoys), to be patted, petted, and photographed in their palaces by their wives, children, grandchildren and their hand-picked ornithologists! The tangled politics of these oil-rich states and the chronic threat of war from without and within would prevent these rulers from meeting in person with only a bird, sorry, they meant to say, with Mr. P.!

Russia offered Mr. P. political asylum and even life residency, provided he changed his name to Pavel Popovich Jr. or Popo for short. If Mr. P. came to Russia under these terms and conditions, he would be housed in a corner shelf of a room in the new Russian Bird Sanctuary Building in Popovich Square, named after and financed by Russia's newest millionaire, Pavel Popovich Sr. (It is rumored that Mr. Popovich made his recent fortune by exporting dancing girls to tired tycoons abroad. Sorry, please excuse my error, I merely meant, of course, that Mr. Popovich made his millions by furthering artistic freedom of expression for freelance Russian dancers by introducing them to appreciative audiences abroad). Moreover, the Russian government also hinted that after a time of naturalization, Mr. P. might be included in at least one space ship's crew for a brief orbital flight around the world. They told Mr. P. that even if he lived in today's Russia of free enterprise, he would be treated **as just another bird** and no opinion of his would ever be allowed private or public expression. Even after a space flight, should such an honor befall him, Mr. P. must merely repeat whatever the flight commander said, down to the last pause or sneeze of that human space hero.

Ecologists from the Galapagos Islands sent Mr. P. effusive greetings, as well as pictures of their famous Blue footed Booby birds. They were genuinely glad that **a** (or should I say, **the**) parrot was the very first recipient of Denmark's **Dahngold Medal of Honor**! They also sincerely hoped Mr. P. would visit their islands at his convenience.

The **International Scientists' Bureau of Antarctica**, busy with penguin preservation, decided <u>not</u> to endanger Mr. P.'s life by inviting him to that icy continent. However, letters of congratulations to Mr. P. were sent by the Bureau. Its members secretly hoped that next year, they, as members of this Bureau, and its honorary members, the penguins, would jointly be awarded **The Dahngold Medal of Honor** for exemplary service to ecology in Antarctica.

After reading and reflecting on all these many messages from the global community, Mr. P. expressed his distaste for most of these offers by using choice phrases from Elizabethan England. "Poltroons' Pavane (i.e. Fools' Dance)! I shall be chilled steel before these scullions!" (Mr. P. had noticed these expressions in the diary of a London lawyer from sixteenth century England. He had found this book in a library in the U.K. where he had done some research). Somehow, these Elizabethan oaths aptly expressed Mr. P.'s umbrage and he felt happier having thus cleared his feathers of this world's dust, so to speak.

Finally the endless news items about Mr. P. were brought to the attention of high ranking government officials in India. They sought to reclaim P., once and for all, by publicly endowing him with India's highest award, the **Bharat Ratna or the Jewel of India** which is bestowed only on a few, rare beings (hitherto only humans) by the President of that ancient land. (As you know, Mr. P. had refused all offers; already mentioned earlier). To everyone's surprise, Mr. P. accepted **this** honor immediately. However, it was Mr. P. who had the last laugh (or should I say screech?) on this occasion! This parrot had long mastered the computer, using his sharp beak to type on the keyboard. Mr. P. emailed everyone who had hitherto contacted him for any reason and invited them to this special ceremony in India's capital during which he would receive the **Jewel of India** award. Floods of visitors, journalists and photographers from every corner of India and indeed the whole world attended this august event while millions watched it on television. Mr. P. used this event to globally publicize the plight of many species, including parrots, who are losing their habitats and are either endangered or facing extinction, due to the loss of forests in India and indeed around the globe. Mr. P. appealed for **world wide Forest Protection laws** and said that he only accepted this prize in order to find a public platform to make this global appeal! Most people were deeply inspired by Mr. P.'s message and even hardened politicians and cynics were temporarily moved by the truth and urgency of **P.'s appeal for**

global Forest Protection laws. The rain forests are the lungs of the Earth, so to speak, and their destruction can only bring incalculable harm to all that lives on planet Earth, including its youngest residents-seven billion people!

Much as Mr. P. loved his native land of India and specially its fading forests, he was in great need of a creative respite from the chaos and continuing crises of this people--centered, human dominated Planet Earth. He knew many countries that are mapped on this planet but Mr. P., like most beings, had never heard of Seagull Island and its Singing Sea. Hearing him weep one night, perched in a fading forest in India, Melisande's mercy welled up within Her and She sent one of the Seagull sentries of Her sanctuary to find and fetch Mr. P.and his loved ones to Seagull Island by magical means. Thus, once again, Melisande's mercy saved some anguished beings from the mainland and restored them to health and laughter.

Let us leave Mr. P. in the safe haven of Seagull Island for the moment and move on to another important topic. What happened next to Ms. B. Grayson of Eugene, Oregon, U.S.A., who was last sighted in Singapore? Let me share with you now some facts about the Grayson, Duckworth and Thistlethwaite families all of whom are either living relatives or wealthy ancestors of Ms. B. Grayson, our distinguished ornithologist. But on second thoughts, it will not be fair to omit other, collateral branches, so to speak, of Ms. Grayson's pedigree, I mean, her family. For example, her granduncle Mr. Braemer Biggleton Bashford, the prize winning pugilist who boxed his way to fame and fortune on both sides of the Atlantic, was the undoubted founder of her family's fortune. When he first arrived in New York in 1921, as an immigrant from a small village somewhere in Europe, his name was Stanlizdh Zgrogd. However, an American immigration officer tried to help Mr. Z. to adjust more easily to this new world. So the officer changed Zgrogd's name to Bashford, when he noticed the huge fists and broken nose of this sturdy pugilist. Later, much later, after many victories in the ring as a prize fighter, this man changed his own name legally to Braemer Biggleton Bashford (on the advice of a Hollywood movie recruiter for stunt men in action films. After retiring from the ring, he did become a stunt man in Hollywood movies for several years before he found his real niche as a highly paid sports commentator for television. He also allowed a young, impoverished graduate student of Anglo-American literature to ghost write his autobiography for a small fee. It was called: *My Feisty Fists: Confessions from the Boxing Ring* by Braemer Biggleton Bashford (the triple B. of Boxing). It was this book which moved him from the ranks of the merely prosperous to the inner sanctum of the fabulously wealthy. After many book singings, readings and reprints of this volume, he finally retired.

Ms. Grayson's Uncle Burr, as he was affectionately called, bought a studio apartment in an elegant part of Boston but still lived out of his one suitcase. His argument, when asked about this habit, was that his happiest years had been spent in rooming houses and later in small, cheap hotel rooms and he saw no reason to darken his golden years (chronologically and financially) by changing his habits. His attorney made it clear to his entire family that Mr. Bashford could have purchased a far less expensive one room apartment in Roxbury, for example, but his decision to purchase this "petite studio flatlette" in a Back Bay basement in Boston was his one and only concession to the snobbery of his grandchildren and their cousins. When Mr. Bashford passed away, each of his surviving relatives inherited one million dollars each, after taxes. His widow was left with ample means for her sunset, I mean, her golden years. However, to everyone's surprise, the bulk of his vast fortune was given to various militant and military organizations both privately run (usually suspected of terrorism by the Establishment) and government run commando units which are always honored and publicly described as "assuring national and global security." His will had clearly stated that in case these privately run militant and military organizations were NOT allowed by the government of either country, his or theirs, from benefiting from his will, that money should then be given to the local police for the maintenance of "attack dogs."

All members of his immediate and extended family decided to further increase his largesse by carefully ransacking their own attics and basements as well as neighboring antique boutiques for "Braemer memorabilia." All these items were auctioned off at gala black **and** white tie social events for large sums of money to Braemer Biggleton Bashford's many wealthy fans both in the U.S. A. and abroad. Many objects, from spoons to ladles, boxing gloves, as well as men's silk gloves with matching neck ties, which were allegedly owned by the famous triple B. of Boxing, were also sold on ebay by members of his family to cyberspace customers who are among B.'s many fans on the world wide web.

Ms. Grayson always publicly expressed her admiration for Uncle Burr by calling him "a pillar of his and our country." She had invested her one million dollars from him into a "nest egg" for senior ornithologists and intended to retire on the income from this fund, the moment she turned sixty five! Did you ever wonder why Ms. Grayson only used the first letter of her first name? She usually asked friends and colleagues to call her "Gray." Her formal documents were always signed B. B. Grayson. You have probably guessed that her parents, wishing to ingratiate themselves with their Uncle Burr (a.k.a. the triple B. of Boxing), had named their only daughter Braema Bashford Grayson! Their loyalty to Mr. Bashford was recognized during his long lifetime in the form of flying visits to their home by this famous uncle and richly rewarded after his death when Mr., Mrs. and Ms. Grayson inherited one million dollars each, after taxes, as you know. Each of these Graysons (and everyone else related to Mr. B.) made, at the very least, another half a million dollars per person, by auctioning off artifacts which had allegedly belonged to their Uncle Burr. (I have already alluded to this matter). Heightened security, both national and global, in the tragic aftermath of 9/11/2001, necessitated that the portion of Mr. B.'s bequest to privately run military and militant groups, could NOT be sent. He had anticipated such a possibility, as you know, and stated in his will that if that happened, the local police station, near his last residence, was to be given a sizeable sum for the maintenance of "attack dogs."

  Did you know that the very first Thistlethwaites to come to America from olde England in 1891 were Sir Thomas and Lady Edith Thistlethwaite and their children Edwina, Edmund and Edward (as well as their butler Mr. Mungo Marston Snodwelks, his wife Lavinia, their five sons, Beresford, Rainesford, Hungerford, Rutherford, Boorsford, Horsely-Hammond and the butler's dog, Cuthbert Mungo Houndsditch-Hammersley, III)? What motivated these distinguished families of Britons to leave Britannia which was then at the height of her global, imperial power, under the august sway and scepter of Queen Victoria herself? The answer is simple—the promise of greater personal prosperity! Sir Thomas Thistlethwaite was to serve as the chief tutor to the (adult) children of a newly rich oil baron from the U.S. heartland who was interested in giving **his** children the quick gloss of the same aristocratic, old-world varnish that the wealthiest, oldest and most snobbish elite of New York society's families with Dutch last names gave **their** offspring! All I need say now is that this experiment was very satisfactory for all concerned and the Thistlethwaites (and even their butler, his family and their dog), lived happily ever after in the U.S.A. Every daughter of that mid-western tycoon (called "oil baron" in common parlance) was eventually introduced to

The Saga of Seagull Island

Queen Victoria herself in London. The reason for these presentations (which occurred with the punctilious observance of every detail of Britain's aristocratic etiquette) is that all three daughters of Mr. Filmer B. Drummond, the aforementioned tycoon, married an impoverished heir to a dukedom or an earldom in Britannia. Thus the trans-Atlantic Anglo-American Alliance was strengthened and heightened to the mutual advantage of these individuals, their families and their countries. In 1897, the Thistlethwaite and the Snodwelk families were given honourable mention in the Birthday Honours List of Queen Victoria, to their great delight and the joy of their employer, Mr. Drummond! One these Thistlethwaites was an ancestor of Ms. Grayson.

The only other families we now need to know something about are the Duckworths and the Graysons. You have already heard Ms. Grayson refer to her cousin the surgeon, Dr. Duckworth of Fla. But the question still remains: Where did the Duckworths come from?

The Duckworths were called Duckworthy in olde England in the village of Ducks 'n Drakes in the county of Deeling in Dorsetshire. In time, the Duckworthys, poulterers for generations, decided to shorten their name to Duckworth, when two of their grandsons became butlers to baronets. In 1880, an American heiress who was touring England with her family met a banker's clerk in London. This man's father, Mr. D. O. Duckworth, was a retired butler who had endowed his children with impeccable manners. In due course, this young lady, Miss Bessie Grote Smith introduced Mr. C. Duckworth , the clerk, to her father, Mr. Groosvert Grote Smith of New York. Impressed by young Duckworth's manners and mercantile skills, Mr. Grote Smith offered him a junior partnership in one of his many companies. Mr. Charles Duckworth promptly accepted this opportunity and sailed to New York with the Smith family in the same ship, although Duckworth traveled in the "steerage" section, while the Grote Smiths went first class. Five years later, Mr. Charles Duckworth and Miss Bessie Grote Smith were married to the delight of both of their families. Thus Duckworth was also added to the illustrious list of the names of those who have strengthened **The Trans-Atlantic Anglo-American Alliance**. Ms. Grayson was specially proud of her Duckworth connection because she loved all birds in general but ducks and parrots were her particular favorites !

The Grayson family itself has a succinct history. One of the Thistlethwaites, Jeremy John Jr., had simply changed his name to Grayson, just before his marriage to a wealthy widow (Mrs. B.F. Grayson or Bonny Betty Grayson) who had met, courted and married him within a matter of weeks. This lady of commanding presence, proven fecundity and ample purse power had easily persuaded this meek, young man (who was fifteen years her junior) to change his name to hers. As far as I know, they had four sets of twins within the first five years of their marriage and lived happily ever after ! Ms. B. Grayson and her cousin, Dr. Duckworth are, of course, the direct descendants of Bonny Betty and Jeremy John (nee Thistlethwaite) Grayson, as well as of Bessie Grote-Smith-Duckworth and C. Duckworth, Esq. So, now you know a great deal about the illustrious ancestry of Ms. B. Grayson, our distinguished ornithologist.

Did you think that Melisande's Seagull Island is simply another seasonless tropical isle, always time-stitched into a sultry summer ? I do hope you credit Melisande with more creativity than that! There are many seasons in Seagull Island, at least six. However, no season ever lingers; so no one becomes bored or is made restless by any period on Seagull Island.

Whenever the mainland increases its sufferings through the follies of its leaders, Melisande decrees a beautiful "snow day" for peace prayers on Seagull Island. The snow there falls as softly and gently as swans' down. Sometimes Melisande creates tiny snow balls which look like miniature, pirouetting, sugar plums and She lets them dance very softly and slowly down to earth. Snow elves skate out of their burrows and mantle the branches of pine trees with delicate, small, snow scarves made of feathery snowflakes. Barren branches and bare twigs suddenly have soft, snow clumps which look like notes of music written on them by celestial composers. The snowfall itself on Seagull Island is as gentle, soothing and smooth as a baby's blanket. Melisande wipes the sky of its usual  colors on these "snow days" and simply shades the sky a snowy mother of pearl, so that it complements in hue, the swans' down snow tones of the island on these days of peace prayers. All islanders of every kind, respect and welcome, these exquisite "snow days" of serenity. The gentle, abundant beauty of these "snow days" fills everyone who experiences this loveliness with a graceful, grateful sense of wonder and a tranquil, mellow joy. On these occasions, one feels as if one has become an organic part of a flute sonata of exquisite beauty and gentle gladness played by a superb, serene musician .

"Snow days of serenity" were not the only days of "peace prayers" on Seagull Island. Regardless of the current season which could be summer, autumn or winter, sometimes Melisande would send an exquisite spring day called "praying with wonder" to this magical isle. Suddenly every tree, bush or hedge would be adorned with the fresh, tender-green leaves of spring. There would be joyous bird songs from choirs of birds who normally return to the mainland in spring but live year long on Seagull Island. Delicate forsythia, daffodils and many colored crocus flowers would be seen everywhere and the grass itself would have the dewy freshness of spring. Moreover, Melisande would be seen dancing a spring polka, covered with the loveliest flowers of this delightful season of Nature's seeming re-awakening to wonder and the re-blossoming of Flora herself. If you enjoy the mainland musicians' odes to spring, then you have heard a faint whisper of Melisande's Spring Symphonies during these "serene days of wonder" on Seagull Island. The Forest of Fairy Folk in Seagull Island had marvelous choirs of fairies and elves whose songs brought joy, wonder and the healing of sorrows to all beings in Melisande's sanctuaries and even a lessening of stress (real or imagined) to humans on the mainland. All beings on Seagull Island delighted in these "spring days of wonder." You will not be surprised to hear that there was a children's choir which included, of course, all the human children of Seagull Island as well as the little birds (or birdlings as they were called). Fawns, baby reindeer, bunnies, chicks and ducklings also joined this group because they loved to dance to the spring melodies of the birdlings and the children's joint choir. There were dancers galore on these "spring days of wonder." It seemed as if all humans and fauna, as well as the fairy folk, and sometimes even the trees and saplings of Seagull Island would dance several rounds of spring polkas with gentle gladness on these "days of peace prayers."

The Singing Sea, the merfolk, the dolphins, the miniature painted fish, the Shape-Shifters and all other residents of the Singing Sea would also gladly participate with music and mirth in these exquisite "spring days of wonder and peace prayers for the mainland" that Melisande mercifully created for the joy of all beings everywhere.

The Seagull Sentries who guarded this isle by flying around it while showering it with music were naturally in harmony with Melisande's " serene days of wonder." Also, their offspring were very helpful to the children's/birdlings choir and taught them melodies that they had learned or were learning from their parents, the Seagull Sentries of this magical isle.

Melisande had requested the Fairy Folk of Seagull Island to provide food, beverages and refreshments of many kinds for **all** beings in Her Sanctuaries on land and sea, on these "tranquil days of wonder." Since Fairy Folk are specialists in magic, as well as the healing arts, Melisande knew that they could nourish all beings in Her sanctuaries without being burdened themselves or missing a single song of celebration on these glorious "days of joyous wonder and peace prayers for all beings everywhere."

The Sky would also help Melisande on these "days of peace prayers for the mainland" by garlanding itself with abundant rainbows. The Sun and Moon would illumine those days with an ethereal radiance and there would be an absence of inclement weather during these "days of special harmony." So you see, Nature and Melisande and all the benign beings in Her sanctuaries did much to help the mainland (or Planet Earth) with their prayers, mirth, music and mercy!

Summer on Seagull Island was a time of glorious abundance of sunlight, songs, flowers, fresh fruits, vegetables and fragrant sea-breezes from the Singing Sea. Tropical birds of vivid plumage were frequently seen here during the summer season, as Melisande's special guests. Forest berries of many kinds, strawberries, raspberries, blueberries, blackberries, gooseberries, a variety of currants and berries unknown on the mainland, grew in succulent abundance in the Forest of Fairy Folk on Seagull Island, as well as in Melisande's other magical Forest of Mirth (which still exists, though time-stitched into medieval France). You can easily imagine, I am sure, how wonderful and indeed wondrous were Melisande's "peace prayer days of summer!"

Autumn, too, was delightfully conducive (as was each season on Seagull Island) to "days of harmony." The glorious painter's palette of Autumn foliage, its reds, yellows, orange, gold, pinks, brown etc. created a natural Symphony of Color on this magical isle. It was against this colorful background that Seagull Island's exquisite, medley of fall melodies were played by Melisande and all Her cherished residents during Autumn and specially during these "fall days of peace prayers for the mainland and indeed for all beings everywhere."

The fifth season on Seagull Island was called Joyful Yellow. It came immediately after summer. For a month, the color of sunlight looked like liquid gold or a very clear honey. People of all ages dressed in yellow during that month. Fruits and vegetables, yellow in color, such as corn, yellow squash and papaya fruit, grew plentifully on that isle at this period. Yellow flowers of many kinds, from exotic, exquisite golden lilies to honey colored roses, filled Seagull Island with their fragrance! Of course, glorious sunflowers were everywhere!

Gentle Rains was the sixth season on Seagull Island. During that month there was a sense of fun and frolic among all the islanders because the raindrops which fell so quietly on the isle were of myriad colors and of many designs and shapes! Sometimes the raindrops, though liquid, looked and smelt like fragrant flower petals. Sometimes the raindrops looked and sounded like notes of music. At other times, the raindrops looked like diamond droplets or a haze of silver or simply like confetti. These magical raindrops sometimes turned into real jewels and at other times, all Seagull Islanders felt as if a cascade of pure joy had just floated into their hearts forever. So, again you can imagine, how easy it was for Melisande to welcome and introduce "days of peace prayers" into the seasons of Joyful Yellow and of Gentle Rains on Seagull Island.

Let me tell you now about the Rainbow Festival on Seagull Island. During the month of Gentle Rains there were five days when the sky above Seagull Island was adorned with rainbows. (You already know about the bounty of the Sky in covering itself with rainbows during the "days of peace prayers," regardless of the season, on Seagull Island). Moreover, for five days, the Gentle Rains on Seagull Island, complemented, in colors, the vivid rainbows of the Sky, above this isle. Every shower of rain would be like a cascade of liquid rainbows. There would also be magical arches and arcs of rainbows all over Seagull Island made of rainbow colored ice, through which all beings could dance, walk or skate, just as they wished! Every puddle was a pool of rainbow colored water which caressed one's feet without wetting them. Every rainbow droplet tasted like one's favorite ice cream. Every fountain which suddenly sprang up all over this island was a glorious swirl of rainbow colored droplets which had the fragrance of flower petals. Children loved to dance through the rainbow colored arches which sang lovely melodies to delight the dancers. At the end of each dance, a rainbow fairy would appear and give each dancer rainbow colored sweets, desserts and other treats which were simply delicious! Even the flowers on Seagull Island became rainbow colored for these five days of the Rainbow Festival, during the Gentle Rains season of mirth. The Singing Sea (whose sweet waters became an exquisite medley of opal-like colors during every twilight hour, as you know), delighted in participating fully during the Rainbow Festival of Seagull Island. For five full days, the Singing Sea time-stitched itself into the sunset hour, so that all beings, whether on sea or land in Melisande's sanctuaries, could enjoy the dazzling splendor of its opaline beauty, at all hours of the day, during the Rainbow Festival of the Gentle Rains season on Seagull Island.

The other main festivals of Seagull Island were the Flower Festival, the Harvest Festival (of delicious vegetables), the Grains Festival, the Forest Festival and the Gardens' Glory Festival. The Water Festival was included in the Rainbow Festival of the Gentle Rains season, for obvious reasons. The other important celebration on Seagull Island was, of course, its Children's Parade during which the offspring of **all** beings on the isle would dance through the main gardens of Seagull Island. Babies, were of course, in their parents' arms, but the parents would dance through these gardens celebrating their infants' presence. The Seagull Sentries' Choir would provide delightful music during the Children's Parade and the Forest Fairies and Elves would join the Children as they danced through the glorious gardens of Seagull Island. The flowers were fine musicians, too, and they would also provide exquisite music, as the Children danced and sang and delighted themselves and everyone else on this lovely day

MARIE'S TALE (the mother of PIP DARCY)

I would now like to tell you something more about the Fairy Folk who live in the Forest of Seagull Island. Like the Mer Folk who live in the Singing Sea, Fairy Folk are usually misrepresented in the stories and myths of the mainland. There is nothing either infantile or sinister about these residents of Seagull Island. The fairies and elves of Melisande's sanctuaries, like the mer folk, are merciful and merry, beautiful and blithe and very benign! The works of fiction that mainland writers create are filled with troublesome gnomes, mischief- making elves, horrible trolls and fairies who are either sweet or sour. I suppose these are figments of humans' imagination and therefore lacking in reality. I have shared with you the facts, as far as Melisande's sanctuaries are concerned. My knowledge is limited to these glorious oases and beyond that my guesses would simply be speculation. So let us stay within the safe precinct of Seagull

Island for the moment and I will tell you what I have seen and also heard from the Fairy Folk of this isle and from Melisande's Will.

One spring morning, I was walking on Seashell Beach when I saw Melisande dancing there with a baby reindeer and a fawn near Her and a snowy, little seagull, with a glowing yellow sunflower in its baby beak, who was sitting on Her smooth right shoulder. No one is ever afraid of Melisande whose mirth and mercy have brought all things to birth and beauty on Seagull Island. But She does evoke awe and adoration! I smiled and watched Her beautiful form swaying to the music of the Singing Sea. Seagull Sentries flew above and around us adding their musical murmur, as Melisande danced at dawn to the cadence of Her Singing Sea. Very soon, a swirl of dolphins were seen gliding and dancing on the silvery waves of the Singing Sea while the Sky above suddenly mantled itself in rainbows to share in this magical morning of Melisande's mirth. Flowers sprang up in the wake of Her footsteps and the sandy Seashell Beach was soon replaced by a vernal green, covered with golden buttercups, daffodils and, of course, the signature flowers of this isle—glorious sunflowers galore! Melisande paused very gracefully and smiled at me. Reading my thoughts easily, She said: "You admire my son, Will, whom most people call Shakespeare. Shall I call my word wizard Will ? He has written about fairies in his plays and you have read and loved his words. Now that you wish to know more about the Fairy Folk of this very isle, I will lend you for an hour, the best wordsmith of all, my marvelous Will." She had barely finished speaking when I saw a cherubic looking child run to Her side. His head was covered with honey colored curls and his eyes had the blue brilliance of the Singing Sea. I had expected to see a balding, middle-aged English yeoman in Elizabethan attire—doublet, hose, with a ruff around his neck and probably carrying a quill pen and parchment, as well as a bottle of ink. At least one portrait of Shakespeare shows a single pearl in one ear, as was fashionable among men at Queen Elizabeth I's court. I had also expected to see a man with russet colored hair and warm brown eyes. If nothing else, I had expected, at least an adult. Instead, here was an adorable child who looked as if he had just stepped out of a Botticelli painting of the Christ child himself. Noticing my surprise the child came to my side and gently said: "Yes, I was William Shakespeare but that was hundreds of years ago. I was sent to the mainland by my mother Melisande as a special boon to people there, not only then but even now when English is spoken globally. No one has written better English or delighted more people with drama and poetry than William

Shakespeare (b.1564-d.1616). But you see my real form now. I am always Melisande's Will, though at times I must use Shape-Shifting to help mortals. I brought back with me the form and garments, I had worn in England as William Shakespeare. I pretended to put a curse on Shakespeare's tomb when I played that part long ago. If anyone had opened or does open that tomb, they will find nothing at all. I can not die for I am a Shape-Shifter and the child of **Melisande, She who has brought all beings and beauty to birth**. Some day, if I tire of Her Creation, I can ask my Mother Melisande to re-absorb me into Her being of mirth and mercy from whence She sang me to birth. But until then, this is my true form. I am Melisande's magical, marvelous Will ! You think I look like a Botticelli painting. That is true, the artist saw me once in a dream when I was sent to inspire him. He was struggling to depict the Christ child for a special canvas at Christmas time. Botticelli never forgot that dream which he called " A vision" and for the rest of his life, he never faltered when asked to paint the baby Jesus or a cherub near that Child." Suddenly Will laughed. His laughter was like a shower of silver bells, lyrical and merry. "Let me tell you about the Fairy Folk of Seagull Island now," he said. " I am so glad this is a simple task, not like the chore of writing plays filled with many plots and sub-plots, histories, romance and drama. The Fairy Folk of this isle are very benign Shape-Shifters who use their magic only for healing and harmony. They are very patient too. You have probably heard that in olden times they helped humans, who were rescued from shipwrecks by the Seagull Sentries, to learn to forget the cruelty and cunning, malice and meanness of their mainland lessons and to become merciful and merry again. Sometimes it took years and years for these rescued mariners to learn the simple joys of caring and sharing. It was the loving-kindness and above all, the patience of these Fairy Folk which brought real healing to these rescued humans! That is why my mother Melisande always gives the Fairy Folk in all of Her sanctuaries, the tasks of nurturing and healing, knowing that they are able to fulfill these duties with grace and gladness and yes, with original goodness, as well." Saying this Will vanished and all I could see was a specially bright silvery sheen on the waves of the Singing Sea, where Will can still be glimpsed at dawn and at dusk.

Thus ends Marie's Tale.

Crispin Quilpen Continues The Saga of Seagull Island

Now let me introduce you to a delightful elf whose name is Meadowlark (a.k.a. Neil on the mainland). He was born in ancient Ireland of Melisande's melody and ever since then he has been (and continues to be) one of her merriest messengers. He loves Ireland and returns there very often, for he can time-travel, as well as journey with ease, quickly and quietly to distant lands. He can also Shape-Shift and time-stitch at Melisande's request, when it is necessary to help beings either in Her sanctuaries or on the mainland. His nick name is Green Thumbs, for Neil is certainly a "master gardener." His flaming red hair inspired Melisande to ask him for a curl with which She painted the first red Autumn leaves in Her Forest of Mirth and the first fall red leaves and berries of the Forest of Fairy Folk in Seagull Island. Some people say that Neil is really a leprechaun, (why else would he be so devoted to the Emerald Isle?), though often he has to work elsewhere, to help and heal, garden and grow sanctuaries where many find hope and happiness. Neil not only enjoys gardening and all things beautiful and blithe in Nature but he also loves to cook. He finds Nature's bounty in his own glorious garden and indeed in all the forests and fields around him on Seagull Island. He had made his own home of aged wood carved with runes and tunes from the Emerald Isle and inside this house there is an inglenook with a glowing fire and an apple kitchen where he bakes and cooks delicious dishes for all the elves and fairies of the forest on Seagull Island. His eyes, like that of Will, have the blue brilliance of the Singing Sea. Once asked why did he not have the dark hair and eyes and the milky skin of the ancient Celts, Neil simply said that he had looked like that, long ago. But in the meantime, Melisande had sent him, a thousand years ago, to quell the Vikings (whose lightening raids from their long ships were a menace to everyone in Ireland and in England, a millennium ago). It was then that Neil decided to invoke his primal coloring from the dawn of Time. Ever since then, he has the brightest red hair and the merriest blue eyes of all the elves in Melisande's sanctuaries!

His orchard has many kinds of apple trees, all bearing fruit which are famous for their flavor and fragrance. Some of the apples are bright red, some are golden in hue, others are in subtle shades of pink and pearl and peach; some apples are petite, some large, others oblong in shape, some are as green in color as the grass of his beloved Emerald Isle but **all** of the apples from Neil's orchard are simply delicious!

Neil's garden has emerald green grass all year long, even in spring, when all other grass on this isle has turned a delicate leaf green color. His green vegetables—peppers, squash, chard, spinach, beans, and broccoli are as green as his grass. Neil, like all elves, enjoys bright hues, so his flower garden is always a lovely medley of colors. Pinks, reds, purples, yellows, white, blue, gold are the colors of his beautiful flowers which are as varied and fragrant, as they are fair. Four leaved clover grows in abundance in his garden, as do many herbs which he uses for medicine to heal beings, as well as to flavor his pot pies, soups and stews.

Let me tell you now about Neil's vineyard. Many kinds of grapes grow there and Neil uses his knowledge, gleaned in ancient Ireland, to make a delightful variety of honey wines. Unlike the mainland, the wine from Seagull Island is never intoxicating or harmful even in excess. Neil is the only islander to make wine here and even Melisande loves and approves of this light, delicious drink called mead (made of fragrant grapes and clover honey) which heightens the alertness and insights of those who partake of this healthful beverage.

Neil's mushroom garden contains many kinds of wholesome fungi which he uses in his salads and soups and sometimes even in his stews. His duck pond always has delightful looking ducks, mallards and ducklings who live as a family, contented and serene. The mother ducks are fond of Neil and often give him their extra eggs for his breakfast or to put in his pies and puddings, cakes and custards. Bunnies, ducklings, chicks, baby reindeer and fawns often visit Neil and enjoy the delicious treats he feeds them. They, in turn, dance on his lawn accompanied by the Birdlings and the Children's choir, to Neil's joy and the delight of all who live in his garden sanctuaries in Seagull Island.

Did you know that Neil, like Will, was lent by Melisande to the mainland for many years to help confused beings there? Neil was sent to a country called Boxland where most people have made themselves miserable in a medley of ways. One of their favorite pastimes is to buy boxes which when plugged into a socket provide them with hours of distraction. They work at various unhealthy and unhelpful tasks in order to receive pieces of used paper which they value as money or the equivalent of gold. Although these bits of dirty looking paper bear no resemblance to that metal, gold, which is so prized in the mainland.

Many of their buildings where they live or work are also shaped like boxes, rather like a stack of boxes, where little squares called rooms, (jealously guarded by these ferocious fools), are regarded as their own expensive homes or prized places of work.

Meadowlark, Melisande's merry elf, Shape-Shifted to become a serious looking business man called Neil, when he was sent to the mainland. Every day, for years he had to drive a metal box with wheels, called a car, far from his rural garden sanctuary (which he had created, even on the mainland) to a distant city. Once he reached that dreary, gray city, he worked in a dark basement of a so-called school run by cruel, cunning, mean and malicious trolls who were masquerading as humans. Neil, too, had assumed human guise but with benign motives. Neil simply wanted to help some members of this motley mainland by remaining a "master gardener" and creating garden sanctuaries of flowers, fruits and vegetables, conserving forests and wetlands and even building a home of aged wood filled with Celtic runes and tunes, an inglenook and an apple kitchen, as he had on Seagull Island. In time, Melisande asked Meadowlark (a.k.a. Neil) to return to Seagull Island, to his great relief and the joy of all islanders who had missed him very much. Before he left the mainland forever, Neil gave his beautiful garden sanctuaries and his exquisite home to a group of benign beings who promised to continue this work of caring and sharing, healing and helping anyone in need. While on the mainland, Neil visited Ireland very often, for he found that such visits to the Emerald Isle helped him to do his difficult tasks of nurturing and gardening in a rare, green corner of Boxland where he had built sanctuaries for the healing of many beings.

Did I tell about Melisande's daughters Melinda and Melissa ? Melinda is a tree nymph who helps the Fairy Folk and all the Elves in the Forest of Seagull Island and in the Forest of Mirth (which is time-stitched into medieval France). Melissa is a sea nymph who works with all beings of the Singing Sea, specially the Mer Folk, the dolphins and the exquisite, painted fish whom you have already met.

Melisande had sung Melinda and Melissa into being aeons ago, just as She had Will and Meadowlark (a.k.a. Neil). All four of Her offspring are Shape-Shifters and benign helpers of all beings in Her sanctuaries and even on the mainland. Will (known as Shakespeare on Planet Earth), has already told us that Melisande's offspring do not die. They can Shape-Shift when necessary and if they ever tire of Her marvelous, motley, medley of Creation, they can always ask Her to re-absorb them into Her being of mercy and mirth (from whence She had sung them into birth). Unlike mortals, Melisande's children do not age, for they are not dominated by Time but can use Time as a tool for benign ends. The problem of Evil which continues to be an enormous issue to mortals on the mainland (a.k.a. Planet Earth) was/is not even a ripple in Melisande's worlds. Why? You may well ask. The reason was/is simple. Melisande's Creation does not have to deal with the hydra-headed, ever-fertile problem of Evil because She (wisely, I think) omitted that germ, when Her mirth brought all beings to birth and beauty into Her sanctuaries long ago. Melisande (again wisely, I think) made Time a tool and not a dominant feature of Her Creation. Hence, time-travel, time-stitching, moving with ease over vast distances with brevity, the lack of an inevitable sequence for the progress of seasons, in short, Her freedom and that of Her Creation from the dominance of Time and the absence of Evil make Her worlds uniquely wonderful.

However, Melisande does not favor idleness and She dislikes lethargy. Hence, there is no lack of many kinds of creative, helpful, healthful work, in which She and indeed all beings in Her sanctuaries, are dynamically engaged. Nature with its myriad beauty and nurturing bounty is Melisande's ally but the baleful aspect of nature which is catastrophic is not admitted to Seagull Island nor to any of Melisande's other sanctuaries, such as the Singing Sea or the Forest of Mirth.

Many fiction writers of the mainland have written about imaginary, idyllic places that do not really exist. Naturally, such authors cannot give satisfactory answers, as to the ways in which these places actually operate. All I can do is give you the facts about Melisande's worlds, based on what I have seen, heard and observed, particularly Seagull Island and the Singing Sea. However, humans in Her sanctuaries were/are not really free from the laws of Time and Nature. The humans in Her oases simply live happier, healthier, longer and more fulfilling lives than they would have on the mainland. I have already told you that it often took rescued mariners (who were brought to Seagull Island after shipwrecks by the magical Seagull Sentries) many years to unlearn the lessons of hatred and to finally learn how to care and share and to live in daily harmony with all that lives. I have also told you that there has not been a shipwreck in the Singing Sea since the sixteenth century. Hence the humans on Seagull Island have had ample time to learn to live in tune with Melisande's melody of mirth and mercy towards each other and with other beings in these sanctuaries.

The humans on Seagull Island were/are farmers and gardeners, builders and painters, cooks and bakers, as well as artists, artisans and musicians. However, as you already know, all humans here were/are taught from childhood, a variety of skills, so that they can all become kind, capable, efficient adults who work well, either alone or in groups, and further develop their knowledge, throughout their lives, in order to help each other. There was/is inter-generational harmony (in these oases of Melisande) and children, their parents and neighbors like and respect each other. Work is not regarded as a burden or a grim necessity but a wonderful opportunity to express one's gifts and ideas in creative, useful and harmonious ways. As you know, there are wonderful seasons and celebrations all year long in Seagull Island and there is accord and respect among species and seasons as well. Humans, in Melisande's sanctuaries, benefit from creative magic but they, like most mortals elsewhere, remain without magical powers. The only beings who know **and** are allowed to exercise magic in Melisande's worlds are (as I have already told you) the Shape-Shifters which include the Fairy-Folk and the Elves, the flora and fauna of Her creation, as well as, of course, Melisande and Her children Will, Meadowlark, Melinda and Melissa. The Singing Sea is, of course, one of Melisande's creations, like the Seagull Sentries. Hence, the Singing Sea, **all** beings in it, **and** the Seagull Sentries are also Shape-Shifters in Melisande's worlds and allowed to use their benign, magical powers.

It will not be difficult for you to imagine what a blessing it is for **all** beings in Melisande's sanctuaries **not** to have to contend with Evil within and around them, as do all the unfortunate beings, specially the humans, on the mainland (i.e. Planet Earth). Just recall a spring day when you felt joyful, youthful, helpful, healthy and truly in harmony with Life! That is exactly how the humans who live in Melisande's sanctuaries feel all the time, as well as all the other beings in these havens!

We now come to the important issues of commerce, law and security etc. What, if any, was/is the currency of Seagull Island and Melisande's Forest of Mirth? What, if any, were/are the rules that govern Her sanctuaries which include, of course, the Singing Sea?

Money, legal and military systems which are considered essential for the governance of countries on the mainland are foreign to Melisande's worlds which, however, flow and function far more ably than the best run states mortals know of, on their planet.

Ages ago, the barter system was used on Earth. Even then, greed and unfairness prevented equal exchanges at all times between humans. Consequently, legal systems which originated as councils of village elders have now become gigantic structures with many branches of law which are differently understood and practiced by diverse nations. Bows, arrows and clubs of ancient days have now "venomed" (this verb is used to mean the opposite of "blossomed") into hydra-headed, "high tech." monsters which can destroy all life on earth.

Many humans on the mainland are exhausted, afraid and oppressed by the power of their own creations which were supposed to make their lives easier, safer and presumably happier e.g. money, law and arms. Yet no one on the mainland knows how to remove these man-made systems from their lives. Some mainlanders have even convinced themselves that only their body's demise will free them from the tyranny of time and evil, as well as from these human creations of commerce, law and weaponry.

Let me return with relief to Seagull Island where I too, mostly live (though I have to exist on the mainland for certain periods, as did Will and Meadowlark, a.k.a. Neil). On Seagull Island, I am delighted to tell you, no one earns money as it is known on earth. Everyone works at many useful tasks which I have already mentioned. There is no dearth of Nature's bounty there. On the other hand, humans and other species still have to actively participate, cultivate and cooperate, in order to enjoy, through caring and sharing, the natural gifts and blessings of Seagull Island. If you have seen a loving family or a caring community on earth, it may give you a small glimpse of the effortless sharing of all resources by the Seagull Islanders. Legal and military systems, deemed essential on the mainland, are irrelevant on Seagull Island. Do you wear a bullet-proof vest and carry a weapon when go to see those you love most? Do you have an attorney and a policeman accompany you when you visit your beloved ? Similarly, living as every Seagull Islander does, in daily harmony with all of Melisande's motley, medley of Creation and in tune with Her melody of mercy and mirth, (and please remember the absence of evil and the lack of time's tyranny in these oases), there is no need here for enforcement of any kind—neither monetary nor through weaponry nor legalities. Consequently, the freedom for which mainlanders yearn, can truly be found fully in Melisande's sanctuaries. Here beings joyfully seek, find, and fulfill their responsibilities to all, rather than start (and continue the cacophony) with a shrill, selfish demand for their own dues, rights and others' duties towards them. By each islander thus willingly, gladly, ably engaging oneself for the harmony and well being of the whole, life on Seagull Island flows like a seamless symphony, for the joy of all and the delight of Melisande.

I would like to show you now some of the wonderful places in the Forest of Fairy Folk on Seagull Island. Sometimes the very word "forest" conjures up a picture of a wood where trees grow densely, blocking out the sunlight and where there are ferocious beasts, as well as poisonous plants, weeds or fungi. Also, forests can be regarded as places of danger for humans, since they are perceived to be dark, ominous, uncharted, trackless terrain, where outlaws and sinister witches and wizards dwell. At least these are ways in which mainland writers often depict forests. Needless to say, the forests in Melisande's worlds were and are very different.

The plight of forests in the mainland, particularly the rapid destruction of rain forests, is a serious concern for thoughtful people on the mainland and for all of Melisande's creations who regard forest destruction as murder. Therefore, forests in Her oases are sanctuaries for the safe continuity of many kinds of fauna and flora who are at risk (or already extinct) on the mainland. I think you will be particularly pleased to know that there are extensive rain forests both on Seagull Island as well as in Her Forest of Mirth. To live in and to nurture these cloud-canopied, rain forests which are filled with medicinal plants and brightly colored toucan birds, (as well as many other kinds of birds, flora and fauna), is the joyful privilege of Her benign Fairy Folk who are also called Shape-Shifters. Regardless of the chaos and carnage on the mainland, Melisande's worlds contain pristine forests and rainforests which are as unspoiled today as they were ages ago. It is in these rainforests that the Fairy Folk find certain plants and herbs which cure the ailments of various creatures, including humans, who dwell on Seagull Island. Bird lovers, for example, will be delighted to know that dodo birds, which are extinct on the mainland, are plentiful on Seagull Island. Also, toucans of large beaks and brilliant plumage are abundant on this isle, as are pelicans, pink flamingos, blue-footed booby birds, vivid red, as well as green plumed parrots and as many other birds as you can name or imagine! If you want to see exquisite dancing peacocks, originally from India, who have found safety in Seagull Island, come to their beautiful sanctuary in the depths of this forest. Of course, the Fairy Folk will admit you, only if they are certain that you come with caring!

Bamboo forests are fading in China, thus the panda's habitat is vanishing and pandas may soon be found only in captivity in the zoos of western nations. In Seagull Island, however, adorable pandas abound in bamboo forests within the larger Forest of Fairy Folk. The koala bear and the kangaroo of the Australian continent, whose habitats are also threatened on the mainland, find safe havens in Melisande's worlds, as do tigers and elephants from India and elsewhere. (Once in Her world, even tigers become peaceful and are nourished by the Fairy Folk without killing other creatures.)

Have you seen the beautiful, emerald green, terraced rice fields of Indonesia? When I first saw them, I marveled at such practical yet lovely landscapes! On Seagull Island, there are such vivid green, terraced rice fields, deep within this forest (and therefore hidden even from the benign humans of this isle who live on Seashell Beach). The Fairy Folk irrigate and maintain these beautiful and bountiful fields which produce rice which has the ineffable, exquisite fragrance of the forests and fields of Seagull Island.

Few, if any, person on the mainland believes in the voices of other species. Yet, in Seagull Island, the Fairy Folk have listened and therefore learned the languages of the birds, the plants, the grains and of course, the fauna and flora, and many other beings in their care, in the forests of Melisande's worlds. Humans who have seized Planet Earth and wrought havoc on the mainland are only one among many species in Melisande's worlds. No human ingenuity can dominate these sanctuaries because (as I have already told you), people, though harmonious in Melisande's worlds, have no access to magical powers. The only beings who can use magical powers in Her worlds are Melisande and the wisest, most benign of Her creations, the Shape-Shifters, the Seagull Sentries and

The Saga of Seagull Island

the Singing Sea and its residents, all these beings who are merciful and merry, beautiful and blithe, just like their Mother Melisande, whose melody of mirth and mercy has sung them into birth.

In spite of the industrial, mechanical encroachment on Nature in the mainland, a few, rare, unspoiled sanctuaries still remain, although no one knows for how long. It was to one of these rare bird sanctuaries, near a tiny wedge of a rainforest, that our ornithologist Ms. B. Grayson had gone,(after her visit to Singapore). One day, she was standing on a rock, at dawn, gazing at the unspoiled beauty of this small sanctuary when she suddenly saw a cave nearby. She only noticed the cave because several brightly colored, very rare birds emerged from it, to her surprise. Very carefully, so as not to disturb these exquisite birds, Ms. Grayson watched the cave from a distance. Two dodo birds, several peacocks, as well as a pair of white peacocks, and two blue footed booby birds, also glided out of that amazing cave. No longer able to restrain her curiosity, Ms. Grayson decided to go to there herself and hoped to photograph more birds, including the ones mentioned above. She was already confident that she would receive the admiration of bird watchers everywhere for the pictures she had just taken of the dodos, peacocks, blue footed boobies etc. As soon as Ms. Grayson crawled into that cave something extraordinary occurred. Suddenly, a shaft of air ejected her through that cave and into the sky. When she opened her frightened eyes, after what seemed to be only a moment, she was standing on the Seashell Beach of Seagull Island to her utter surprise and delight!

What had occurred was simply this—on rare occasions the Fairy Folk return some of the mainland birds to their original homes, if there is a safe sanctuary for them there. The Fairy Folk assure the birds that if they find themselves in any danger, they have only to fly into the sky and call and the Seagull Sentries will instantly bring them back to Seagull Island by magical means. Though very happy on Seagull Island, these birds have occasionally felt nostalgic for the mainland which is why they were brought back to this bird haven by the Fairy Folk. However, Ms. Grayson, had accidentally fallen into the tail wind of these Fairies and now here she was in Seagull Island itself!

Dawn near the Singing Sea is certainly a wondrous sight. Ms. Grayson was experiencing awe and delight and only a twinge of surprise (but not fear) when she saw a woman walking briskly towards her. She did not know that this was Melisande's daughter Melinda, an exquisite nymph of Her forests who is also a very benign

Shape-Shifter. Melinda now looked like a middle-aged ornithologist, complete with binoculars, bifocals and field notes. On approaching Ms. Grayson, Melinda was able to be reassuring and helpful without disclosing the magical nature of the isle. She was able to persuade Ms. Grayson that this was a privately owned island and that she had accidentally experienced their latest form of "high tech," airborne flights. This argument may not have convinced Ms. Grayson or anyone else on the mainland. However, Seagull Island's luminous beauty has the magical effect of bringing inner joy and peace to anyone who enters this isle. Ms. Grayson was shown some parts of the rain forest to her great delight, after which Melinda in her new guise of a mainland colleague, persuaded Ms .Grayson to walk through a certain woodland arch of the Forest of Fairy Folk. In a moment, Ms. Grayson found herself safely back in the bird sanctuary she was visiting, before her strange sojourn to Seagull Island. Subsequently, Ms. Grayson never alluded to this adventure in her public discourses but in her field notes she wrote that she had gone briefly to a private estate where there was considerable emphasis on conserving natural habitats, based on ecological principles.

You may well wonder what happened to Mr. P., that remarkable parrot from the fading forests of India, who had achieved great erudition in the field of **eco-jurisprudence** which had then led to his global fame. Happiness requires but a brief statement while agony, conflicts, tragedy etc. can and do contain endless pages of literary or legal descriptions.

Mr. P., as you know, was/is neither melodic nor mystical but a logician and a lawyer. However, he wisely decided to make his permanent home in Seagull Island with his few relatives. Enjoying the care and company of the magical Seagulls, Mr. P. is there now and will probably live there happily ever after. True to his legal training, Mr. P., stated to the Seagull Sentries and even to Melisande that he was voluntarily changing his status from "Honored Guest" to "glad resident" of this isle. Mr. P. feels that he has done all he could to help the mainland and his responsibility now is to live and learn about the principles of caring and sharing which are the keys to the success of sustainability of Seagull Island. I have italicized the essence of the long, legal statement that P. has written, defending (though no one challenged him) his decision to live on Seagull Island, where, as you know, money, legal systems and weapons are irrelevant, since the entire sanctuary lives and flows very harmoniously (and efficiently), based on Melisande's melody of mercy and mirth, caring and sharing, with all beings in the motley, medley of Creation.

I would now like to tell you about some other festivals which were celebrated on Seagull Island to the great joy of the islanders and the delight of Melisande. Every year during spring, Melisande sends a message to the pandas of Seagull Island who live in the bamboo forests deep within the Forest of Fairy Folk,(as you already know). A very special Spring Festival (which coincides with the Chinese New Year on the mainland) is celebrated annually in the bamboo groves, for the delight of the pandas in particular and the Fairy Folk in general. Of course, humans and other species on this isle are always cordially invited but this spring celebration is the special favorite of the pandas who hold fond memories of their ancestral habitats in China.

The elders/mentors of the pandas of Seagull Island are Wu-wei and Feng-shui who are considered sages by the other pandas who know that they can always depend on this couple for clarity, compassion and sound advice. Wu-wei (which literally means "doing nothing") is a wise Taoist. He looks to the flow of benign natural rhythms for counsel. Water, for example, though gentle and fluid, can, in time, erode the hardest stone. Again, water takes the form of the vessel into which it is poured. However, the power of water has been proven (even by modern scientists on the mainland) and we all know that humans, flora and fauna cannot exist without water. The composition of the human body, as well as of Planet Earth, indicates the importance of water to a great extent. Hence, Wu-wei is correct in regarding water as an important teacher in his life.

Even his name, Wu-wei ("doing nothing") requires a word of explanation. In the modern world of the mainland, the emphasis is on haste and swift results which have been the cause of much of its sorrows and sufferings. This fragile blue planet now faces ecological crises created by short-term goals such as the rapid destruction of the rain forests and the pollution of the air, water, and oceans in many parts of crowded and war-torn Earth.

"Doing nothing" or Wu-wei, according to ancient Chinese wisdom teachings, is flowing in harmony with the cadence of Nature, thereby living harmoniously with Life.

Feng-shui is a term difficult to describe. Again, according to ancient Chinese wisdom teachings, it means finding and placing oneself (and one's possessions) in harmonious ways, in order to find beauty, health and happiness, by flowing with the cadence of Life.

Wu-wei and Feng-shui had both been born in China but had wanted to live in a serene and secure place which was not threatened by pollution and human industrial activity. They had been brought to Seagull Island by magical means, for Melisande had heard their cries. These two pandas and their descendants are living very happily in a bamboo forest, deep in the heart of the Forest of Fairy Folk on Seagull Island.

Family life, in an extended sense, was valued by the ancient teachers of China and this concept is one that many Chinese humans, as well as the pandas of Seagull Island, still hold dear. From time to time, other pandas have also been rescued from the mainland and now there is a contented colony of pandas happily dwelling in the delicious bamboo groves of this magical isle. These pandas are now serene, secure from harm and with an abundance of bamboo for their food, fresh water and good company. Knowing how very much these pandas love Nature and the nature mysticism (or some would say the practical, nature-based teachings) of Lao-tse, the sixth century B.C.E. sage of ancient China, Melisande invites Lao-tse's spirit to the Pandas' Spring Festival every year.

The tangible bodies of humans, flora and fauna, die, of course, but the souls of the truly wise continue to light the path of many beings, long after these teachers have physically passed away. That is why it was/is possible for Melisande to invoke and invite the essence or spirit of Lao-tse whose soul dwells in the realm of Pure Light. On hearing Melisande's song , every spring Lao-tse's spirit assumes the form of an elderly man and he comes for a week to inspire and gladden the pandas of Seagull Island with his presence and his example. Every dawn, for those seven days, the pandas gather on the gentle slopes of a green hill, near their bamboo groves and they watch the sunrise with Lao-tse, who sits in their midst. Then, Lao-tse opens his famous, brief book *The Way of Wisdom* or *Tao te Ching* which he had written with brush and ink on rice paper long ago (at the request of a young guard when Lao-tse was leaving the imperial city and its library where he had worked for many years, for retirement in the Chinese countryside, 2,500 years ago).

The ancient teachings of China emphasize reverence for departed ancestors whose spirits are regarded as deathless. That is why, there is no element of surprise or fear among the pandas when they sit near the spirit of Lao-tse, every spring, for a week and hear him read from The Way of Wisdom. The pandas of Seagull Island, under the benign guidance of Wu-wei and Feng-shui (whom they regard as their Grandparents and as Wise Elders), are so in harmony with Lao-tse's teachings that they do not have to ask anything of him during his annual visits. They rejoice in the sage's presence and they are inspired by his readings which make his well-known book dawn-fresh to them and help to deepen the pandas' love of wisdom and their delight in following Lao-tse's teachings in their daily life.

As you know, it is usually not possible to be a follower of several religions, in a literal sense, concurrently. However, it has been possible for the Chinese people of ancient and even of modern times to appreciate concurrently (I must use that word again) the wise teachings of Lao-tse, Confucius and the Buddha. You may be interested to know that the sixth century B.C.E. is sometimes called the "axis age" because several great instruments of wisdom were dwelling on Earth during that time. Lao-tse and Confucius were living in China, the Buddha in India, Zoroaster in Persia (today's Iran) and the Hebrew prophets, Jeremiah and Isaiah in Israel!!!

Many Chinese people, both in the past and in the present, find solace in Buddhism when they face disease, old age or death, either in their own lives or in that of their loved ones. Confucius' teachings provide, for many Chinese, an invaluable guide to maintaining peaceful relationships with fellow-humans in a wide variety of settings and circumstances. Lao-tse taught the way of wisdom by observing the benign forces of Nature. The pandas of Seagull Island are sentient beings (as are all beings in Melisande's oases). So you will not be surprised to learn that the pandas of Seagull island are cognizant of the wisdom teachings of ancient China which they regard as their heritage, as well as being deeply appreciative of and in harmony with, the benign melody of Melisande's mercy and mirth which pervade Her worlds.

Every year during the month of May on the mainland which sometimes coincides with the season of Joyful Yellow in Seagull Island, there is another Spring Festival for the joy of the pandas, the peace of all beings on Seagull Island (and on the mainland) and the luminous gladness of Melisande Herself.

This Spring Festival coincides with the birthday celebration of the founder of Buddhism on the mainland, just as the Pandas' Spring Festival (which I have just described) coincides with the celebration of the Chinese New Year.

According to ancient Buddhist legend, the royal infant who would become a world teacher was born on a full-moon night in May in a garden. Melisande knows that Her music can inspire Great Souls (who dwell in the realm of Pure Light), to manifest themselves occasionally on Seagull Island, for the peace of the Universe. So you will not be surprised to learn that every year, the pandas of Seagull Island and indeed all the residents of that isle, see an immense shaft of light on the Buddha's birthday. The already peaceful islanders experience an ineffable peace and joy, as they gaze on that Luminous Immensity. Then, there is a gentle shower of fragrant, yellow petals which melts into light, as it reaches the ground and everyone on the isle is reminded by the Panda Elders about the Buddha's sermon, **The Secret of the Golden Flower**. (At least on one occasion, during his earthly life, the Buddha did not preach but simply gazed at a golden flower which he held in his hand during that hour of silent meditation). Consequently, this celebration is called the **Golden Flower Festival** on Seagull Island which coincides with the Buddha's birthday celebrations on the mainland.

In the fall, the pandas of Seagull Island, celebrate **Ancestors' Day**. They do not invoke the spirit of Confucius who has asked them to follow his teachings of social harmony but to allow his essence to remain in the realm of Pure light. However, the spirits of all their other ancestors are invoked and after thanking all their past and present teachers and guides, the pandas of Seagull Island have a wonderful afternoon of storytelling, followed by a banquet of fresh bamboo shoots and spring water. Wu-wei and Feng-shui then lead all the pandas in a special dance that they had learned in their youth in China. This dance, in honor of the Bamboo Groves, is accompanied by delicate flute music, (the flutes, of course, are made of bamboo). So now you see that pandas are not giant toys but sensitive, sentient beings who enrich Seagull Island by their wise and wonderful presence.

You may well wonder whether the humans on Seagull Island have any religious celebrations? As I have already told you, there has not been a shipwreck off Seagull Island since the sixteenth century and the human islanders and their children live in a peaceful atmosphere of caring and sharing with all beings in Melisande's sanctuaries. However, the rescued mariners (whose descendants are the human islanders) were Christians. Or I should say, Christianity was the official religion of the pirates who manned those ships. As you already know, it was the patient, loving-kindness of Melisande's Fairy Folk which gradually taught these mariners to care and share and sometimes it took them many years to unlearn the violent lessons of the mainland. However, in honor of the human islanders' ancestral religion, there is a glorious Christmas on Seagull Island every year with carols galore from the Children's and Birdlings' Choir accompanied by music from the Seagulls and the Singing Sea. Easter is celebrated in the spring, at the same time as the mainland. There is a marvelous profusion of many kinds of fragrant lilies all over Seagull Island during Easter and all beings there feel a deep sense of awe and wonder as they celebrate the blessings of that sacred season.

C. S. Lewis's *Voyage of the Dawn Treader* describes the beauty of the "last sea" in the "utter east" which is covered with lilies and whose waters taste sweet. Monet's paintings of water lilies inspire many people with their ethereal loveliness. These works and classical compositions of music which reflect the cadence of dancing flowers give humans a glimpse of the bounty and beauty of the lilies of Seagull Island. Traditional white, trumpet-shaped Easter lilies, exquisite cream colored lilies which look like they have white lace embroidery on their petals, calla lilies, vivid red, "Asiatic" lilies, orange "tiger" lilies, salmon pink, magenta, burgundy, scarlet, "shocking pink," sunlight yellow, baby pink, peacock blue and gold are but some of the shades of the lilies of Seagull Island. Lilies here are truly amphibious flowers, for they can be found covering the Singing Sea (specially at Eastertide) as well as displaying their multi-colored splendor on the green meadows and gently sloping hillsides of Seagull Island, until all one can see is a mantle of fragrant white and gloriously colored, floral magnificence!

The signature flowers of Seagull Island are sunflowers and lilies of every variety. Roses do grow here, as do jasmines, gardenias, tube roses, **parrot tulips**, daisies, as well as many other kinds of flowers. But the most popular flowers of Melisande's sanctuaries are definitely sunflowers and lilies. Indeed, one of Melisande's many names is "The Lily of Hope and Purity." She is also called "Sunflowers' Spring" for it was Her prayer which evoked the lily into being and her smile which brought the sunflower to birth.

You may well wonder who Crispin Quilpen, the author of this book is . In the mainland, writers introduce themselves at the very beginning of their books. Their pictures are frequently on the book's jacket and there is often a writer's introduction, before the book even starts. My purpose in writing this *Saga of Seagull Island* is simply to acquaint the reader with Melisande's sanctuaries which are full of Her mercy and mirth, music and harmony.

Moreover, Melisande's marvelous Will (who is known on the mainland as William Shakespeare) thought it would be interesting for the readers of this saga to know something about its author. Will forgot to do this when he was a prolific author of plays and poetry in Elizabethan England (where he was lent and sent by Melisande). Even today, there is so much speculation and controversy about the identity of William Shakespeare.

Will was laughing the other day when I saw him on Seagull Island's Seashell Beach. He said that the only possibility that mainland scholars (who are still discussing his life and works) have not yet stumbled upon, is the truth—that he is still alive and well on Seagull Island where he can be seen at dawn and dusk as a silvery sheen on the Singing Sea. Will is a benign Shape-Shifter who cannot die as he was sung into being by his mother Melisande who alone can re-absorb Will into Her being, if he ever tires of Her motley, medley of marvelous Creation.

Crispin Quilpen's Tale

I was brought into being aeons ago when Melisande's laughter created Seagull Island and most of its inhabitants. I enjoy, as does my friend Will, being a silvery sheen on the Singing Sea. Sometimes, Melisande asks me to assume a form, to render Her a service. Therefore, I have occasionally become an exquisite, "painted fish," dwelling inside the beauty of the Singing Sea. When I have been sent to the mainland (a.k.a. Planet Earth) I have usually chosen the form of a mouse, a small, cosy, warm creature which easily avoids human detection and ownership. When Will was lent to England for fifty two years (1564-1616) and became William Shakespeare, Melisande asked me to accompany him. Since we were companions, we lessened each other's burdens on this long sojourn. As a mouse, (though fully cognizant and able to speak, think and act clearly), I could live in Will's pocket by day and sleep in a hole in his room by night. It was I who found stray feathers of birds and sharpened one end of a feather with my teeth to create quill pens for Will, (who needed many a quill pen then). It was I who found the ingredients for ink and using magic, ground and diluted them to create legible, flowing ink for Will (who used gallons, or so it seemed) to write his plays and poems.

It was I who could fly, easily and often, (changing my form from mouse to moonbeam), back to Seagull Island, to take Will's news to Melisande and bring him many messages from home. It was I who would frequent the Mermaid Tavern, the English shipyards, even Queen Elizabeth I's court and her inner chambers,(invisible to human sight), to keep Will fully informed of "breaking news" and secret information from every quarter. No wonder scholars of Will's plays are still amazed that a glover's son, a country lad who was only a player, could know so much about history and politics, psychology, and the machinations of royalty etc. We ShapeShifters from Seagull Island, Will and Crispin, worked well together, to make that long sojourn of fifty two years in England, a real success!! No one has yet surpassed Shakespeare's literary genius and now that English is spoken globally, millions of new readers from every country and every clime are discovering and marveling at the literary legacy of William Shakespeare. Yes, those long, cold, adventure-filled years of our joint exile/sojourn did and does help many humans.

My real name is Spring Joy, as Will's actual name is "Melisande's marvelous Will." However, neither of these names could be used on the mainland, so Will became William Shakespeare (i.e. one who shakes a weapon to stop evil-doers but who does not use a spear to wound anyone). It was Will who suggested the name Crispin Quilpen for me. I love this name and I still use it when I have to communicate with humans from the mainland. One winter's evening, Will finished writing the now famous, rousing speech to his soldiers by King Henry V in which "St. Crispin's Day" is mentioned. Suddenly, Will put down his quill pen and laughed. He said: "Odsbodikins, (an Elizabethan oath), I do believe I finally have a name that will suit you, friend Spring Joy. Does the name Crispin Quilpen find favor with you?" (In those days, people's trades or professions were often used as their last name, e.g. Baker, Glover, Taylor, etc.). I was really pleased with this new name and thought how apt it was (and is) for me. There is little joy in the hearts of most people on the mainland and their spring is often brief, cold and rainy. So how can they really resonate with my real name, Spring Joy? But Crispin Quilpen conjures up a quaint English name with a Shakespearian ring and describes my craft of pen making, as well.

I must confess that I inspired Beatrix Potter when she wrote the story about the *Tailor of Gloucester* (who was helped by mice who made a wedding coat with beautiful embroidery for the Mayor). I also inspired C. S. Lewis to create Reepicheep, the

the valiant, talking mouse of Narnia. When literary people are looking for symbols from the world of Nature, we Seagull Islanders sometimes help them by sending them a waking dream or a vision by night when they are asleep. Remember how Will once appeared to Botticelli in a vision when the painter was struggling to depict the Christ child? However, after catching a glimpse of Will's true form, (the child of Melisande), Botticelli's cherubs and baby Christs always had Will's honey colored curls and his eyes which reflect the benign, blue brilliance of the Singing Sea.

What task, you may well ask, am I engaged in now ? I thought I would attempt the impossible. I thought I would try to depict with words, the beauty and bounty, the music and mirth of Melisande's sanctuaries and give you a glimpse of our life on Seagull Island. Will has retired from writing, believing that his task now (through his compassionate presence), is to be a source of enormous love and light to all beings. So, now it is my humble duty to Melisande to be the modest bard and chronicler of Her wondrous worlds, Seagull Island and its Singing Sea as well as Her Forest of Mirth (which is time-stitched into medieval France, as you already know).

I could have told you many a hair-raising tale of our sojourn in Elizabethan England and also our years in the reign of James I. But I have decided not to include any tale, episode, incident or adventure that you have already gleaned from history books or literary works. My sole purpose in writing this Saga is to share with you the wondrous worlds of Melisande.

As I was writing this Saga, inside a cosy, tree hollow, in the Forest of Fairy Folk on Seagull Island, a baby seagull just brought me a message from Melisande with a gift of a gloriously golden sunflower from Her. She wants me to tell you something about Will's sojourn in England and then she hopes I will conclude this tale with some further glimpses of our life here on Seagull Island. I am always glad to receive Melisande's wise counsel, for I am her child, as well as the chronicler of her wondrous worlds.

Let me only say that Will was fascinated by the problem of evil on the mainland and its many manifestations. In play after play, sonnet after sonnet, Will depicted the problems of lust, greed, anger, obsession, war, excessive passion etc. All this you already know. Will was like a child who discovers knives but unlike a child who can easily cut itself, Will, like a circus knife thrower, deftly worked with the many issues of evil without becoming injured in the conjuring process. Melisande protected Will from becoming seduced by evil or by secular fame. Will's mission was to warn humans of the dangerous power of passion and the pitfalls of evil. He led a very simple life while on Planet Earth. I know this since I was his close companion. All I can say is that when our sojourn was finally over and Melisande asked us to return to Seagull Island, there was a look of rapture and radiance on Will's face which was sadly absent during his laborious life in England. Since his return to Seagull Island, Will has refused all offers to return to Planet Earth. He has put away forever his adult garb, his ink, quill pens and parchment and is happiest being a silvery sheen on the Singing Sea, helping Creation through the light of his compassionate presence, rather than assuming a mortal form again.

Let me now reiterate some important features of Melisande's wondrous worlds which I have already shared with you in this Saga. The germ of evil was wisely excluded by Melisande when She created Her sanctuaries. Her worlds are also free of the dominance of time. Therefore, the six seasons of Seagull Island do not have an inevitable sequence. Hence, time-travel, time-stitching are benign options for Melisande and Her creatures. I have found it difficult to describe in English, the time flexibility of Melisande's worlds. Let me call it the "continuous present" which includes, of course, the present as well as the immediate and the distant past.

Money, weapons and law-enforcement are irrelevant in Her worlds, for reasons I have already mentioned. Yet, there is neither boredom nor idleness in Her worlds where all beings live in harmony with each other and in rhythm with Her dominant music of mercy and mirth. All beings in Her sanctuaries work willingly with each other, in order to access the bounty of Nature, without excess or exploitation of Nature's gifts. Humans on Seagull Island are NOT the dominant species but merely part of the orchestra of many other species. Melisande Herself has said that as a species, humans are the youngest and least wise of Her Creation.

If you can imagine a beautiful spring dawn or a summer morning when you felt joyful, hopeful, idealistic and willing to care and share the blessings of Life with all those around you, then you will have a glimpse of the genuine gladness and music of our life on Seagull Island. We are not here to barter or haggle but to willingly, joyfully love and live in harmony with all of Creation. We think of ourselves as an orchestra and Melisande as the wise conductor of this symphony of melody, mercy and mirth, of caring and sharing with all beings, in a circle of luminous harmony.

Here ends The Saga of Seagull Island.

POSTSCRIPT

This ***Saga of Seagull Island*** was commissioned by Melisande in the season of Joyful Yellow and written by Her bard and chronicler, Spring Joy (a.k.a. Crispin Quilpen and Shuma Chakravarty) and concluded on the last day of the aforementioned season of Joyful Yellow on Seagull Island, April 23, 2013, on Planet Earth.

April 23 is St. George's Day in England and the birthday of William Shakespeare, my once and continuing friend, "Melisande's Marvelous Will.." Will now lives on Seagull Island and can be still be seen at dawn and at dusk, as a silvery sheen, on Melisande's Singing Sea.

WISHING ALL BEINGS PEACE AND JOY

AMEN

Reflections
Candles of Hope

Perspectives
from the diaries of

Shuma Chakravarty
and
Crispin Quilpen

Reflections

Balancing her water jug, a woman and a camel are mirrored against the mystical backdrop of the Taj Mahal.

Unlikely allies - a bird is perched on a zebra in South Africa.

*Perspectives
from the diaries of*

Shuma Chakravarty
and
Crispin Quilpen

ENDINGS AND BEGINNINGS

This is both an epilogue to my book *Take Joy* and a prologue to my next book *Reflections*.

I wish to thank my editor Craig Smith for his technical and administrative excellence. This book was first published in 2013 by Converpage. Special thanks to Pamela McCallum.

Lewis Carroll's *Through the Looking Glass* is a wonderful example of reflections in the literal sense. However, I regard reflections as meditations. Due to many problems in the last three years--- global, national and personal, I have not yet completed a smiling sequel to *Take Joy*.

However, the beautiful photographs of Nature donated by photographers (who wish to remain anonymous) will give the reader a glimpse of the joyful vistas *Reflections* will explore.

The following two poems which I will now share with you are my reflections on grief. But they are candles of hope as well. Why? Both poems reflect my conviction that the Divine One is the Center and Source of everything.

Two Reflections

To God

*I asked for Death
That I may have
Peace at last.*

*You gave me
A quizzical glance
And Your opal chalice
To quaff ---
A goldfish draught
Of incandescent joy
And vivid pain.*

*"Shuma, do small things with
Great Love. Do something beautiful
for God"*
        *St. Mother Teresa
        (b.1910 - d.1997)*

God's Grace

*Sometimes this seems
A winter world of woe
Where widows' solace
Lies in green-gold
Memories of their
Brief bridal.*

*So is it with the Soul.
Here midst the frost-
Freckled meadow of
My mind, only
Memories,
Memories of
Your grace remain.
Your glad bounty
To my maiden heart.*

*Your grace?
My mead, my Lord
And myrrh.*

CANDLES OF JOY

There have been golden glimpses of God's grace that have embraced me all day, like a mantle of light. It is then that the chaos and clutter of existence fall off and what remains is the luminous grace of Life. I agree with the English poet William Blake "If the doors of perception were open, then man (sic) would see everything as it is -- Infinite."

This is written in December 2016 which is the Season of Glad Tidings
in Seagull Island by Rev. Shuma Chakravarty (a.k.a. Crispin Quilpen).
Wishing all beings Peace and Joy.

Crispin Quilpen

P.S. - The picture on top of the first *Reflections* page is that of St. Mother Teresa and Rev. Shuma Chakravarty (taken in Kolkata, India in 1993)

www.ingramcontent.com/pod-product-compliance
Lightning Source LLC
Chambersburg PA
CBHW081254170426
43198CB00017B/2790